Transient Worlds

Also by Arthur Sze

POETRY

Into the Hush
The Glass Constellation: New and Collected Poems
Sight Lines
Compass Rose
The Ginkgo Light
Quipu
The Redshifting Web: Poems 1970–1998
Archipelago
River River
Dazzled
Two Ravens
The Willow Wind

TRANSLATIONS

The Silk Dragon II: Translations of Chinese Poetry
The Silk Dragon: Translations from the Chinese

PROSE

The White Orchard: Selected Interviews, Essays, and Poems

EDITOR

Chinese Writers on Writing

Transient Worlds

ON TRANSLATING POETRY

Arthur Sze

POET LAUREATE OF THE UNITED STATES

LIBRARY OF CONGRESS
WASHINGTON, DC

COPPER CANYON PRESS
PORT TOWNSEND, WASHINGTON

Cover art: Ik-Joong Kang, *Moon Jar Dialogue with Moon Jar,* detail, 2016.
Mixed media on wood, 48 × 48 in (121.9 × 121.9 cm).

Published by Copper Canyon Press, in association with the Library of Congress

Copper Canyon Press is in residence at Fort Worden State Park in Port Townsend, Washington, under the auspices of Centrum. Centrum is a gathering place for artists and creative thinkers from around the world, students of all ages and backgrounds, and audiences seeking extraordinary cultural enrichment.

LIBRARY OF CONGRESS CATALOGING-IN-PUBLICATION DATA
Names: Sze, Arthur editor
Title: Transient worlds : on translating poetry /
Arthur Sze, Poet Laureate of the United States.
Description: Washington, D.C. : Library of Congress, 2026. |
Summary: "An anthology of global poetry in translation edited by
25th United States Poet Laureate Arthur Sze, published in association
with the Library of Congress"— Provided by publisher.
Identifiers: LCCN 2026001481 (print) | LCCN 2026001482 (ebook) |
ISBN 9781556597329 paperback | ISBN 9781619323315 epub
Subjects: LCSH: Poetry—Translations into English | LCGFT: Poetry
Classification: LCC PN6101 .T734 2026 (print) | LCC PN6101 (ebook)
LC record available at https://lccn.loc.gov/2026001481
LC ebook record available at https://lccn.loc.gov/2026001482

9 8 7 6 5 4 3 2 FIRST PRINTING

COPPER CANYON PRESS
Post Office Box 271
Port Townsend, Washington 98368
www.coppercanyonpress.org

To Michael Wiegers

Contents

Foreword

FOR MORE THAN EIGHTY YEARS, THE LIBRARY OF CONGRESS has appointed US Poets Laureate (formerly called Consultants in Poetry) to advocate for the literary form by bolstering the Library's collections, developing programs, and leading outreach efforts. The role has evolved to include an optional signature project, ranging from Billy Collins's set of 180 poems designed to be read during school announcement periods to site-specific poetry installations in seven different national parks throughout the country, launched by Ada Limón. No matter their approach, each laureate has found compelling ways to say: Poetry is everywhere and poetry is for us all.

A number of laureates have edited poetry anthologies based on their signature projects, and anthologies by the last three laureates have been published in association with the Library of Congress during their appointments. But this book is the first to focus on poetry translation, as twenty-fifth US Poet Laureate Arthur Sze examines and celebrates the power of translating poems from around the world and throughout history.

Sze has said that he learned the craft of poetry by first translating ancient Chinese poems. In *Transient Worlds: On Translating Poetry,* Sze gives readers the same opportunity. He opens the book with three translations of the poem "Drinking Wine" by Chinese poet Tao Qian, also including the poem written in Chinese characters with their literal translations, inviting readers to try their own translation.

To those who know Sze—a longtime professor at the Institute of American Indian Arts, and the inaugural poet laureate of Santa Fe—and his work, such an open invitation exemplifies what he brings to his current position. His is a poetry of openness, expansiveness, and making new connections. Writing poems and translating poems are for Sze acts of faith in the ways language grows and adapts to continue imagining ways of being. As he says in his introduction, "Great poetry ignites and reignites our shared humanity over time, and the transient worlds of poetry in translation play a vital role in bringing us together."

If this book sparks your curiosity in its source texts, or other poetry, I hope you take the opportunity to engage with the resources and collections of the Library of Congress. They can inspire you just as they inspired Arthur Sze, who wrote the poem opposite after our librarians introduced him to treasures from our collections. The Library can connect you to transformative sources of knowledge and creativity, whatever your interests may be.

Robert R. Newlen
Acting Librarian of Congress

Library of Congress

You peer down a lit corridor
on the fifth tier of stacks
where a million books breathe
on shelves; here's a book
on neutrinos captured in Antarctica,
here's another on solar flares.
A curator displays a book
in Vai script and points to a triangle
with two dots; you wonder
if you are looking at a pregnant
woman, an enslaved man,
or a human ear; you pull a book
off a shelf and, opening it,
hear *Del aire al aire, como*

then snap it shut: the air hums
with honeybees. A second curator
points at glittering gold script;
though you can't divine a word,
you guess *Farsi* and dive
into the marlin-blue depth of the page.
A third curator shows you 心遠
woodblock printed on mulberry paper,
and as you read *a distant mind*
leaves the earth around it,

you smell daylilies in a courtyard
and know you may caravan
to Timbuktu, but there's no
pear-blossom end to what's within reach.

Introduction

I HAVE LONG REFLECTED ON THE QUESTION *How can we deepen our understanding of poetry?* In each of my twelve poetry collections, in each poem and each line, I have explored the malleability of language—writing in and adopting words from English, Chinese, Japanese, Hopi, and Spanish. This exploration was furthered through my translation work as I carried meaning from classical Chinese poets to today's readers of English-language poetry. Then, in the classroom setting, I discovered how this meaning-making within and across languages can spark the creativity of students. In over two decades of teaching at the Institute of American Indian Arts in Santa Fe, New Mexico, I developed a class called "The Poetic Image." There, I walked students through classical Chinese poems, character by character, line by line, included several translations in English of the same poem, and invited Native students to translate ancient Chinese poems into English and sometimes into their own Native languages. The translation work and ensuing discussions were crucial in helping students develop their own voices and visions as poets writing in English.

Transient Worlds has been fashioned as a guide for widening and deepening the appreciation of poetry through the lens of poetry in translation. Here are poems in Arabic, Braj Bhasha, Chinese, Danish, French, German, Greek, Hebrew, Japanese, Navajo, Russian, Spanish, and Tzeltal, with accompanying translations and discussions. When I first started translating poems from classical Chinese into English for *The Silk Dragon,* I wrote out each poem character by character, stroke by stroke, so that I could personalize the process of creation inside each poem and carefully consider how one character was selected and then juxtaposed with another. I discovered that translation is the deepest form of reading. I had to slow down and engage in exegesis, and that step is only the beginning. A good translation draws on cross-cultural understanding, and the language has to come alive. If a translation sounds like a translation, you have failed in your effort. A good translation appeals to our ears, eyes, and heart; it is a singular endeavor and a humanizing act that makes the ancient contemporary, the foreign accessible, and the emotional, intellectual, and spiritual music of the human interior universal.

Transient Worlds is not organized as a linear narrative with a beginning, middle, and ending; instead, it is organized into zones. Each zone is a creative exploration of translation and is rooted in a particular poem or poems. If you read through the zones consecutively, you will discover the conversations are interconnecting, and you can single out particular zones of interest to return to. If you have an interest in Surrealism, you can start with Pablo Neruda in Zone 8, jump to Aimé Césaire in Zone 11, and go on from there. If you are interested in classical Greek poetry, you can start with Sappho in Zone 7 then go to the *Iliad* in Zone 5. If you are interested in visual poetry, you can start with Apollinaire in Zone 4 then go to Orlando White in Zone 2. And if you are interested in Asian poetry, you can start with Tao Qian in Zone 1, go to the opening chapter of the *Tao Te Ching* in Zone 3, then move on to Issa's haikus in Zone 6. I have designed the zones to be interpollinating: Moving through this book in any sequence, you will see the manifold possibilities of translation emerge, and your understanding of what translation is and can be will deepen.

Translation, indeed, is everywhere; and English, a composite and growing language, has been enriched and strengthened over time by accruals from languages across the world. The word *translate* comes from Old French, and even further back from the Latin *translatus,* meaning "to bring over, carry over." So, we might find literary translation to be a process of carrying over all the sound and sense of an original poem into a new language. But then the Italian phrase *traduttore, traditore* comes to mind. This cliché—"translator, traitor"—suggests that a translation is an inferior version of the original, that because it cannot carry *all* of the original, it is unfaithful to it. Now, if a translator attempts the impossible task of bringing a poem from one language into another without loss, they might well betray the meaning and intention of the original poem; but if the translator recognizes the many possibilities for meaning that this carrying-over affords them, they will embrace the process of transformation and renewal that *is* translation, and better reflect the original's networks of meaning.

As language is always evolving, speech patterns, syntax, and vocabulary always shifting, translations are by nature ephemeral. A good translation of a poem finds a voice and shape of language that is fresh and invigorating. This book begins by looking at a poem by Tao Qian (Tao Yuanming), who lived in China from 365 to 427 CE, presented in its original Chinese characters, with Pinyin phonetic spellings and words in English under each character. Three different translations of the poem follow, and the discussion shows how the translators worked in English to create their effects. At the end of this zone of study, readers are invited to make their own translations.

Each subsequent zone takes a different approach to translation and presents a poem—in a different language and written sometimes in a different era—for discussion. For example, in Zone 5, we examine a famous passage from Homer's *Iliad.* How is an ancient Greek epic translated and transfigured when a poet treats the original poem as source material to excavate and write through? We will juxtapose Robert Fagles's translation with the opening of Alice Oswald's book-length poem *Memorial.* Oswald's creative translation presents us with a catalogue of Greek warriors who died in the Trojan War within the *Iliad*'s timeline and goes on to employ many Homeric and oral-tradition techniques that give life to the warriors named, killed, and passed by in the original work. Oswald's poem is an act of reclamation, founded on translation but not bound by it, and her expansive vision is a translation of the highest order.

In Zone 9, we will watch the poet with the magical pseudonym Búffalo Conde channel the voice, spontaneity, and tone of poems written over two thousand years earlier in another language. We'll see what happens when a biblical source, the Song of Songs, written in Hebrew, finds its way into Spanish, then into the Mayan Tzeltal language, and then again into English. Isn't this evidence that the pathways through translation are surprising and endlessly pollinating?

In Zone 10, a poem by Marina Tsvetaeva is translated from Russian by Elaine Feinstein and by Carol Moldaw. Moldaw does not know Russian, but she reached out to a friend who read the Russian aloud, and together they worked through the poem. Their translation process is spelled out in detail in this zone, and, at the end, the reader is invited to reach out to someone—a relative, a teacher, a friend—who might help them make a translation from a language they have little knowledge of.

Translation practice is a vehicle to develop our own poetry; and to write poetry, with its sonnets and sestinas, its haikus and ghazals all carried over into English from other languages, is to awaken to the possibilities—and expand the resources—of our shared language. Translation, after all, builds bridges and makes connections. The more we give, the more everyone has. Great poetry ignites and reignites our shared humanity over time, and the transient worlds of poetry in translation play a vital role in bringing us together.

I hope this book, by including so many varied approaches to literary translation, can widen and deepen our experience of and pleasure in reading poetry. To support the use of this book in classrooms and for individual study, I have included an appendix with supplemental translation- and poetry-writing prompts. What is more, I hope *Transient Worlds* will circulate through our communities a recognition of our shared, intertwined cultural history. I invite you readers, poets, translators, and students of all languages to revel in the power of words: to craft your own translations and to write poems inspired by the creative act of translation.

Transient Worlds

ZONE 1

TAO QIAN (TAO YUANMING)

Drinking Wine (V)

結	廬	在	人	境
jié	lú	zài	rén	jìng
build	*hut, house*	*at, in*	*people*	*region*
而	無	車	馬	喧
ér	wú	chē	mă	xuān
and, yet	*without*	*carriage/s, cart/s*	*horse/s*	*noise, clamor*
問	君	何	能	爾
wèn	jūn	hé	néng	ĕr
ask	*you*	*how, why, what*	*can*	*be*
心	遠	地	自	偏
xīn	yuăn	dì	zì	piān
heart, mind	*far, distant*	*place, earth*	*naturally, self*	*remote, secluded*
採	菊	東	籬	下
căi	jú	dōng	lí	xià
pick, gather	*chrysan-themum/s*	*east/ern*	*hedge, fence*	*below, by*

悠	然	見	南	山
yōu	rán	jiàn	nán	shān
distant, remote	*thus, so*	*see*	*south*	*mountain/s*
			South Mountain	

山	氣	日	夕	佳
shān	qì	rì	xī	jiā
mountain	*air*	*sun-*	*set*	*fine, beautiful*

飛	鳥	相	與	還
fēi	niǎo	xiāng	yǔ	huán
fly/ing	*bird/s*	*each, another*	*with*	*return, go back*

此	中	有	真	意
cǐ	zhōng	yǒu	zhēn	yì
this	*in*	*there is*	*true*	*meaning, sense of things*

欲	辨	已	忘	言
yù	biàn	yǐ	wàng	yán
wish, want	*distin-guish*	*already*	*forget, overlook*	*word/s, speech*

Drinking Wine (V)

I built a cottage right in the realm of men,
yet there was no noise from wagon and horse.

I ask you, how can that be so?—
when mind is far, its place becomes remote.

I picked a chrysanthemum by the eastern hedge,
off in the distance gazed on south mountain.

Mountain vapors glow lovely in twilight sun,
where birds in flight join in return.

There is some true significance here:
I want to expound it but have lost the words.

translation by Stephen Owen

Drinking Wine (V)

I live here in this busy village without
all that racket horses and carts stir up,

and you wonder how that could ever be.
Wherever the mind dwells apart is itself

a distant place. Picking chrysanthemums
at my east fence, I see South Mountain

far off: air lovely at dusk, birds in flight
going home. All this means something,

something absolute: whenever I start
to explain it, I forget words altogether.

translation by David Hinton

Drinking Wine (V)

I built my house near where others live,
and yet without noise of horse or carriage.
You ask, how can this be?
A distant mind leaves the earth around it.
I pick chrysanthemums below the eastern fence,
then gaze at mountains to the south.
The mountain air is fine at sunset;
flying birds go back in flocks.
In this there is a truth—
I wish to tell you, but lose the words.

translation by Arthur Sze

TAO QIAN (365–427), ALSO KNOWN AS TAO YUANMING, was a poet who always felt constrained by official appointments. He once worked as libationer for his district but soon resigned. He was then offered a job as keeper of records but turned it down. Eventually he moved to a rural area, planted chrysanthemums, wrote poetry, and celebrated the joys of drinking wine. His contemplative style became known as "fields and gardens," and in Chinese history he is an exemplar of someone who is true to himself and follows his own path.

In the early 400s, Tao Qian composed twenty wine-drinking poems, and he says in a preface that they were not written with a single coherent vision in mind. Instead, he assembled them loosely around this theme. "Drinking Wine (V)" is one of his most memorable poems, and I've included the original with current Pinyin spelling below each Chinese character, along with a word or a few words in English. You can see the poem is ten lines long and has five characters to each line. In this form, pauses are predetermined, so that the line is read 1-2 / 3-4-5, where the slant line marks the caesura. The line is rhythmically asymmetrical, in that one reads two characters and then three. The Chinese language has four tones—level, rising, dipping, falling—and the Pinyin diacritical marks give a clue to the tone. I say clue, because surely the sounds of these characters have changed dramatically over time. It is said that contemporary spoken Cantonese is closer than spoken Mandarin to how the characters would have sounded in Tao Qian's time.

In the first translation, by Stephen Owen, you can see that he's taken the compact ten lines of Tao Qian's poem and chosen to use a couplet form in English. Each of his lines is end-stopped, so the pauses in his translation follow the pauses in the Chinese, and the stanza breaks help initiate turns or movements. It is rare in Chinese poetry for a poet to use the pronoun *I*—it feels egocentric to use *I,* though the later poet Li Bai (701–762; see this book's appendix) is an exception and has a few famous instances where he asserts the power and presence of the self—and in this poem it feels natural for the *I* to be omitted. Interestingly, Stephen Owen's translation relies heavily on *I* by opening the first three stanzas with that pronoun, and the last line also asserts the presence of the speaker with "I want to expound it but have lost the words."

One important distinction between poetry in the East and poetry in the West is the place of the self. In Song-dynasty landscape paintings, there are often huge mountains and waterfalls, and near the bottom of the scroll is a bridge, and a tiny man headed toward that bridge. There is a sense of people's place being very small in the larger scheme of things. In Western poetry, the self is often foregrounded, so it's important for a translator of Chinese poetry into English to consider the relationship between self and nature.

In David Hinton's translation, you can see that he's also chosen to use couplets, but here they are not all end-stopped. The ends of enjambed lines create pauses or moments of tension before moving on to the next line or stanza. David Hinton's translation has a very different rhythmical flow than Stephen Owen's. And look how different the phrasing is! Stephen Owen's last line, with "expound" as the first verb, features an *I* who has touched on a fundamental truth and wants to explain and enlarge on this insight; at least that's the reverberation I find in that unusual word choice. David Hinton's ending, "whenever I start / to explain it, I forget words altogether," also has a definitive ring to it. The adverb "altogether" has the quality of a summation or dismissal.

You can obviously go through these two translations, line by line, phrase by phrase, to see different decisions each translator has made, and I invite you to do so. I'm adding a third translation, my own, as another lens through which to look at and experience this poem. In line 3, the motion of the language is clearly toward a question, and Stephen Owen renders it, "I ask you, how can that be so?" David Hinton removes the question and makes that passage an assertion, "and you wonder how that could ever be." I lean toward Stephen Owen here and render that line as "You ask, how can this be?" Also, I like the compression in Tao Qian's poem and I believe these consecutive one-syllable words work well.

In Chinese, when one names the four directions, one says, "east, south, west, north." I suggest that Tao Qian's poem, by turning through three of the four directions, enacts a form of centering. In the landscape of the poem, chrysanthemums are located by the eastern hedge and mountains to the south—or there could also be a specific place, South Mountain—and then the speaker sees birds flying back in the west. In this turning from east to south to west, the speaker centers himself and has an insight and feeling of deep truth. This moment comes as the speaker contemplates north. In China, winter storms come out of the north, and this last unnamed direction imbues the poem at this juncture with a sense of mortality. The speaker discovers that when he tries to put this insight into language, it is immediately lost. I try to personalize this sense of loss by inserting a comma and translating the last line as "I wish to tell you, but lose the words."

These three translations present contrasting ways of experiencing this poem, and all three are worth careful consideration. Offering the poem in Chinese characters, along with clusters of words in English, and with these three translations as a guide, I invite readers to try their hands at making their own translation into English.

ZONE 2

ORLANDO WHITE

Duality

hózhǫ́ = for balance

hóchxǫ' = for imbalance

HERE IS A POEM IN NAVAJO (Diné) by Orlando White. Rather than call "Duality" a one-word poem, I prefer to call it a visual, compound-word poem. The poem contains two Diné words, with the second word inverted, and the two words pivot around the letter *o.* The acts of translation occur in the gloss, and what a different language and culture the Diné world is from the European world! The Diné have a ceremony for celebrating a child's first laugh. What would our society be like if we had something similar? Where European languages tend to center around the verb *to be,* the Diné language centers around the verb *to go.*

In any language, a single word may have so many meanings that it is untranslatable, and that is certainly the case with *hózhǫ́. Hózhǫ́* is frequently translated as beauty, balance, or harmony, but it means so much more. Harry Walters, who served as the director of the Diné College Museum from 1973 to 2008, says that *hózhǫ́* involves a state of beauty where everything is good, and where everything interconnects. By including interconnection, Harry Walters shows that *hózhǫ́* embodies a vision of the cosmos, of all that exists, and that the spiritual world and physical world are interconnected and even one and the same. And yet, as we know that disruption in life, in the world, occurs again and again, so Orlando White's poem presents that truth by tipping the compound word. *Hózhǫ́* is right side up, and *hóchxǫ́'* is inverted. The visual poem shows a world atilt, a world in flux, and some of the power of this visual poem is that the microcosm of a word becomes a macrocosm.

NOTE: Many Americans know the Navajo people for their work as code talkers during the Second World War, where they aided American troops by communicating in a language the Japanese could not understand. *Diné* means "the people," and I have used *Diné* when referring to the language and culture and *Navajo* when looking in from the outside.

ZONE 3

LAO TZU

Tao Te Ching, Chapter 1

道可道,
非常道。
名可名,
非常名。
無名天地之始;
有名萬物之母。
故常無欲,
以觀其妙;
常有欲,
以觀其徼。
此兩者同,
出而異名,
同謂之玄。
玄之又玄,
衆妙之門。

I

The way that can be spoken of
Is not the constant way;
The name that can be named
Is not the constant name.
The nameless was the beginning of heaven and earth;
The named was the mother of the myriad creatures.
Hence always rid yourself of desires in order to observe its secrets;
But always allow yourself to have desires in order to observe its
manifestations.
These two are the same
But diverge in name as they issue forth.
Being the same they are called mysteries,
Mystery upon mystery—
The gateway of the manifold secrets.

translation by D.C. Lau

1

The way that becomes a way
is not the Immortal Way
the name that becomes a name
is not the Immortal Name
no name is the maiden of Heaven and Earth
name is the mother of all things
thus in innocence we see the beginning
in passion we see the end
two different names
for one and the same
the one we call dark
the dark beyond dark
the door to all beginnings

translation by Red Pine

I

Tao can be talked about, but not the Eternal Tao.
Names can be named, but not the Eternal Name.

As the origin of heaven-and-earth, it is nameless:
As "the Mother" of all things, it is nameable.

So, as ever hidden, we should look at its inner essence:
As always manifest, we should look at its outer aspects.

These two flow from the same source, though differently named;
And both are called mysteries.

The Mystery of mysteries is the Door of all essence.

translation by John C.H. Wu

I

A Way called *Way* isn't the perennial Way.
A name that names isn't the perennial name:

the named is mother to the ten thousand things,
but the unnamed is origin to all heaven and earth.

In perennial Absence you see mystery,
and in perennial Presence you see appearance.
Though the two are one and the same,
once they arise, they differ in name.

One and the same they're called *dark-enigma,*
dark-enigma deep within dark-enigma,

gateway of all mystery.

translation by David Hinton

TAOISM (DAOISM) IS AN ANCIENT CHINESE PHILOSOPHY and religion that shows people how to find balance and live in harmony with the cosmos. Its principal text, the *Tao Te Ching,* usually translated as *The Way and Its Power,* was composed by Lao Tzu around 500 BCE. I say composed, but there is some question as to whether Lao Tzu even existed. Lao Tzu means "old sage," and D.C. Lau, who was chair of Chinese Literature at the Chinese University of Hong Kong, suggests that Lao Tzu was not a historical figure at all and that the *Tao Te Ching,* comprising eighty-one chapters, is a compilation by an editor or even series of editors. We will probably never know, but the *Tao Te Ching* is a seminal text and over two hundred translations into English exist.

The opening chapter presented here in Chinese is remarkable for its rhythm, its incantatory spell, and its lean power. The character 道 is composed to two parts: The main component refers to "head," while the dot and running line, following traditional organization of the language according to 214 radical or root elements, is radical 162. I think of this radical as a foot running, and it means "to run" or "to go." I like to think that the character suggests that following the Way is not possible through the mind or intellect alone; rather, the mind and body working in unison, like yin and yang, enable harmony. It's important to note that in contrast to Tao Qian's poem, written in poetic form with five characters to a line, here the number of characters per line varies. Three of the opening six characters are 道, and three of the next six characters are 名 ("name"). In ordinary conversation, we repeat sentences to make sure our meaning is clear, but here repetition creates a spell and is a form of insistence. It doesn't make sense to include Pinyin spelling as a guide for pronunciation for such an ancient text, so I have omitted it.

For this zone, I've selected four excellent translations of the opening chapter. In the first translation, D.C. Lau harnesses the repetition in the Chinese—"way" is used twice, and "name" is used three times—while keeping the meaning in English clear. As the Chinese text lengthens, from three characters a line to six, Lau's translation struggles a bit to carry the meaning into English without making the phrasing stiff. The dichotomies of "hence always" and "but always" sound awkward to my ear, but he articulates those distinctions well with "These two are the same / But diverge in name as they issue forth." His translation also closes beautifully with "Mystery upon mystery— / The gateway of the manifold secrets."

We see immediately that Red Pine's translation is more concise than D.C. Lau's. In the opening lines, "way" and "name" are each used three times, and this follows the Chinese. Where the Chinese lines lengthen, D.C. Lau's dichotomy, "rid yourself of desires" and "allow yourself to have desires," is radically transformed with Red Pine's "innocence" and "passion." Red Pine's articulation of separation and union is effective with "two different names / for one and the same." His removal of punctuation also creates a subtle feeling that everything is open-ended. And the closing, "the dark beyond dark / the door to all beginnings," is lucid and lovely.

John Wu's translation employs a stanzaic structure to give the assertions some weight and then some ensuing silence. Where the lines lengthen in Chinese, Wu chooses to syntactically foreground "hidden" and "manifest" by moving those phrases near the beginnings of lines 5 and 6, whereas Lau uses "secrets" and "manifestations" at the ends of lines 7 and 8. When Wu comes to the passage of separation and union, his rendition is effective: "These two flow from the same source, though differently named." The verb "flow" helps erase the boundary. And, at the end, Wu gives much more weight to the closing phrase by using "Mystery" and "Door" and by making a one-line stanza: "The Mystery of mysteries is the Door of all essence."

In looking at the first three translations and then reading David Hinton's, it's fascinating to see how a Chinese character that was translated as "constant," then "immortal," then "eternal," now becomes "perennial." Hinton, like Wu, opts for a stanzaic structure, and I find his second stanza effective and moving. The Chinese text uses "ten thousand things" to describe all that exists in the world, and Hinton adheres closely to the Chinese with "mother to the ten thousand things."

Toward the end of the chapter, it's interesting to see how Lau's "mystery" is rendered as "dark" by Red Pine, then "Mystery" by Wu, and then "dark-enigma" by Hinton. The first three translations are pretty close to one another, but Hinton diverges by coining a special term, *dark-enigma,* for the Chinese character 玄. Certainly 玄 is used many times in the *Tao Te Ching,* and a translation of this character as dark, mysterious, and profound only scratches the surface. Chinese etymologists agree that 玄 contains "silk" in the part of the character below the horizontal line. I have a theory that the character depicts indigo dyeing: The silk hangs from a pole into a dye vat. This may seem fanciful, but indigo dyeing works by oxidation. When silk is pulled out of a dye vat into air, the dye reacts with oxygen and the silk fibers turn blue. With repeated dippings and liftings, the silk gets bluer and bluer, a condition known as blue-approaching-black. Two thousand years ago this chemical process must have been mysterious and profound. One year while teaching at the Institute of American Indian Arts, I had a Japanese student who agreed to the meanings I've listed, and then she added her own; she defined 玄 as "almost disappearing."

While this discussion of a single Chinese character may seem like a digression, I want to circle back now to touch on the sense of mystery that pervades the opening chapter of the *Tao Te Ching.* Unlike a dialogue in Plato where characters intellectually struggle to define an abstraction such as "Truth," the opening lines of the *Tao Te Ching* feel palpable and insistent, with a grounded sense of mystery. In that way, 玄 is an important lens through which to see this language.

ZONE 4

GUILLAUME APOLLINAIRE

L'Oeillet

que cet œillet te dise
la loi des odeurs
qu'on n'a pas encore
promulguée et qui viendra
un jour
régner sur
nos cerveaux
bien +
précise & + subtile
que
les
sons
qui
nous dirigent
Je Préfère ton nez
à
tous
tes
organes ô mon amie
Il est le trône de
la
future
SA
GES
SE

The Carnation

May this carnation tell you the law of odors which has not yet been announced and which one day will come to rule in our minds far more precisely and more subtly than the sounds which guide us
I prefer your nose to all your organs O my love. It is the throne of future knowledge

translation by Roger Shattuck

GUILLAUME APOLLINAIRE (1880–1918) was a poet, playwright, novelist, and art critic. In 1917, in program notes for *Parade,* a ballet that was a collaboration between poet Jean Cocteau, composer Erik Satie, and painter Pablo Picasso, Apollinaire coined the term *Surrealism* to promote their new kind of work. As a poet, Apollinaire was inventive, playful, and full of imaginative risk. If you read "Le Pont Mirabeau" ("The Mirabeau Bridge"), gorgeous for its clarity and sound harnessed to lament love's passage over time, you would not expect the same poet to write "Zone" ("Zone"). In this latter poem, places and times shape-shift, and surprising juxtapositions happen again and again. I've named the sections of this book "zones" in honor of Apollinaire.

Here is another visual poem, this time in French. Apollinaire composed many, and they were published posthumously in 1918 in the collection *Calligrammes.* The word *calligrammes* is a portmanteau, constructed by splicing two words together; it appears to come from "calligraphy" + "pictogram." Apollinaire wrote visual poems in the shapes of falling lines of rain, a heart, and even the Eiffel Tower. The poem here is part of a three-part composite poem, "The Mandolin, the Carnation, and the Bamboo," in which the pieces are arranged to form a kind of triangle. The poems are handwritten, with the words in various sizes. Apollinaire himself called these poems "visual lyricism," and, in 1918, he asserted they were written at the dawn of a new era that would see the rise of film and the phonograph.

When you look at "The Carnation," what is your reaction?

Visual poems are sometimes denigrated as a cheap trick, and yet visual poems have existed in many literatures and in many epochs. A poet is, etymologically, a maker, and poems are constructed out of words. George Herbert titled a poem "The Altar," having spaced its words to create the eponymous shape. Dylan Thomas wrote poems in diamond and hourglass shapes, and Inger Christensen wrote a poem in the shape of a ceramic vase. In this poem, Apollinaire's creative play is apparent, and he also displays humor: "I prefer your nose to all your organs O my love." I like how the poem is oriented toward the future, "the law . . . which one day will come to rule in our minds," and how it engages the senses of sight, sound, and smell. The carnation, the poem's visual shape, is invoked as the vehicle by which a reader-viewer will come to learn "the law of odors." And "it," the nose, is the "throne of future knowledge." I would have rendered "SAGESSE," at the bottom of the poem—whose capital letters emphasize its importance—as "WISDOM," but translator Roger Shattuck has chosen "knowledge." In addition, Shattuck abandons the visual elements of the original poem and renders his translation in prosaic form.

In the poem's absence of punctuation, in its visual arrangement that calls attention to the poem as artifice, as a work composed of words, and in its pointing toward the future, Apollinaire has provocatively created a moment in time.

ZONE 5

HOMER

Iliad 8.542–565

Ὣς Ἕκτωρ ἀγόρευ᾽, ἐπὶ δὲ Τρῶες κελάδησαν.
οἳ δ᾽ ἵππους μὲν λῦσαν ὑπὸ ζυγοῦ ἱδρώοντας,
δῆσαν δ᾽ ἱμάντεσσι παρ᾽ ἅρμασιν οἷσιν ἕκαστος·
ἐκ πόλιος δ᾽ ἄξοντο βόας καὶ ἴφια μῆλα
καρπαλίμως, οἶνον δὲ μελίφρονα οἰνίζοντο,
σῖτόν τ᾽ ἐκ μεγάρων, ἐπὶ δὲ ξύλα πολλὰ λέγοντο.
κνίσην δ᾽ ἐκ πεδίου ἄνεμοι φέρον οὐρανὸν εἴσω.
Οἳ δὲ μέγα φρονέοντες ἐπὶ πτολέμοιο γεφύρας
ἥατο παννύχιοι, πυρὰ δέ σφισι καίετο πολλά.
ὡς δ᾽ ὅτ᾽ ἐν οὐρανῷ ἄστρα φαεινὴν ἀμφὶ σελήνην
φαίνετ᾽ ἀριπρεπέα, ὅτε τ᾽ ἔπλετο νήνεμος αἰθήρ·
ἔκ τ᾽ ἔφανεν πᾶσαι σκοπιαὶ καὶ πρώονες ἄκροι
καὶ νάπαι· οὐρανόθεν δ᾽ ἄρ᾽ ὑπερράγη ἄσπετος αἰθήρ,
πάντα δὲ εἴδεται ἄστρα, γέγηθε δέ τε φρένα ποιμήν·
τόσσα μεσηγὺ νεῶν ἠδὲ Ξάνθοιο ῥοάων
Τρώων καιόντων πυρὰ φαίνετο Ἰλιόθι πρό.
χίλι᾽ ἄρ᾽ ἐν πεδίῳ πυρὰ καίετο, πὰρ δὲ ἑκάστῳ
ἥατο πεντήκοντα σέλᾳ πυρὸς αἰθομένοιο.
ἵπποι δὲ κρῖ λευκὸν ἐρεπτόμενοι καὶ ὀλύρας
ἑσταότες παρ᾽ ὄχεσφιν ἐΰθρονον Ἠῶ μίμνον.

Iliad 8.630–654 (translator's line numbering)

So Hector urged his armies. The Trojans roared assent.
The fighters loosed their sweating teams from the yokes,
tethered them by the reins, each at his own chariot.
They herded cattle out of the city, fat sheep too,
quickly, brought on rations of honeyed, mellow wine
and bread from the halls, heaped the firewood high
and up from the plain the winds swept the smoke,
the sweetness and the savor swirling up the skies.

And so their spirits soared
as they took positions down the passageways of battle
all night long, and the watchfires blazed among them.
Hundreds strong, as stars in the night sky glittering
round the moon's brilliance blaze in all their glory
when the air falls to a sudden, windless calm . . .
all the lookout peaks stand out and the jutting cliffs
and the steep ravines and down from the high heavens bursts
the boundless bright air and all the stars shine clear
and the shepherd's heart exults—so many fires burned
between the ships and the Xanthus' whirling rapids
set by the men of Troy, bright against their walls.
A thousand fires were burning there on the plain
and beside each fire sat fifty fighting men
poised in the leaping blaze, and champing oats

and glistening barley, stationed by their chariots,
stallions waited for Dawn to mount her glowing throne.

translation by Robert Fagles

from *Memorial: A Version of Homer's "Iliad"*

The first to die was PROTESILAUS
A focused man who hurried to darkness
With forty black ships leaving the land behind
Men sailed with him from those flower-lit cliffs
Where the grass gives growth to everything
Pyrasus   Iton   Pteleus   Antron
He died in mid-air jumping to be first ashore
There was his house half-built
His wife rushed out clawing her face
Podarcus his altogether less impressive brother
Took over command but that was long ago
He's been in the black earth now for thousands of years

Like a wind-murmur
Begins a rumour of waves
One long note getting louder
The water breathes a deep sigh
Like a land-ripple
When the west wind runs through a field
Wishing and searching
Nothing to be found
The corn-stalks shake their green heads

Like a wind-murmur
Begins a rumour of waves

One long note getting louder
The water breathes a deep sigh
Like a land-ripple
When the west wind runs through a field
Wishing and searching
Nothing to be found
The corn-stalks shake their green heads

by Alice Oswald

WE HAVE NO RELIABLE INFORMATION ABOUT HOMER (eighth century BCE), and it is unlikely that there was such an actual person. If there were, he was blind and was clearly the heir to a tradition of oral poetry. His own term for *poet* is *singer.* The *Iliad* depicts the Trojan War and is an exploration of heroic code; wrath (the opening word), war, and brute force are foregrounded. Each era has its translation or set of translations that carry over this epic of 15,693 lines, recorded in dactylic hexameter, and here translation becomes a vehicle for carrying forth history and shared human experience. Translations in this lineage are forms of extension and renewal.

I've selected one of my favorite passages from Fagles's translation of the *Iliad.* Earlier in book 8, Zeus forbids the gods from interfering in the battle to come, so a contrast between divine control and human vulnerability is set up. In the quoted passage, Trojans are camped on the plain at night, and their campfires are bright against the dark landscape. The only Trojan mentioned by name is their hero, Hector. The other warriors, referred to as "the men of Troy," are nameless. In the hours before dawn, before battle with Greek warriors, "when the air falls to a sudden, windless calm," there's a restraint and a particularity of detail that are powerful and moving. The oncoming battle hangs in the air, and none of the warriors knows who will live and who will die. Winds sweep up the smoke from the campfires, and the sweet aroma of honeyed wine lifts into the sky; then there's a Homeric simile that expands across seven lines. The simile begins with "as stars in the night sky," then opens into a landscape with a pastoral vision that includes a shepherd, and closes off with "so many fires burned." A reader or listener would have looked up into the night sky only to look down onto Earth to see the stars become the campfires on the plain. It's a magnificent passage, with the stallions "champing oats / and glistening barley," awaiting battle in daylight.

In 2011, British poet Alice Oswald published a book-length poem, *Memorial*, which she subtitles "*An Excavation of the 'Iliad.'*" In her introduction, she notes that she is translating the *Iliad*'s atmosphere and not its narrative. Up to now, I have been looking at translations with an eye to some form of fidelity, where you can, say, look at the original Chinese characters and consider how different translators have chosen to render that poem or passage into English; but translation consists of so much more than carrying the text over from one language to another. AI can quickly make a mechanical translation, but it is devoid of emotion and spirit. Genuine translation is humanizing and involves imaginative transformation and renewal. In *Memorial,* Alice Oswald uses many Homeric techniques to excavate the text at hand. She begins with a catalogue, a list of Greek warriors killed in battle according to the *Iliad*'s timeline, and the list begins with Protesilaus and ends with, beyond this excerpt, Hector. Where the *Iliad* mentions the name of a warrior and little else, Oswald draws on the *Iliad* but is not bound by it. Here creative acts of translation and transformation breathe life into the interstices of an ancient text, and she reclaims warriors who in the original text have little more than their names.

Protesilaus is the first Greek to disembark the ships. Oswald draws on information from Homer, so that Protesilaus has "forty black ships" with men he has brought from his kingdom in Phylace, their places named in a mini-catalogue, and she has the aura of Homer when she describes Protesilaus as a "focused man who hurried to darkness." "Hurried to darkness" and "flower-lit cliffs" are wonderful, mythic descriptions. Then, instead of following the narrative of the *Iliad* by describing how Protesilaus lands on shore, then fights and kills several Trojans before he in turn is killed by Hector, Oswald gives him the equivocal line "He died in mid-air jumping to be first ashore." The word "died" is equivocal, because, on the one hand, Protesilaus wants to be first to get to shore and is "dying" to do so, while, on the other hand, according to prophecy, the first warrior to land on the shores of Troy will be first to die; but Oswald has him dying "in mid-air" before he has even landed. Oswald continues with two nine-line stanzas, each containing two Homer-inspired similes, "like a wind-murmur" and "like a land-ripple," that carry the wind of oral tradition into her original poem. This vision of Protesilaus, and the vision of *Memorial,* is original, vitalizing, and transforming.

ZONE 6

KOBAYASHI ISSA

Three haikus

Uguisuya Doroashinuguu Umenohana

うぐいすや どろ足ぬぐう 梅の花

Upon the blooming plum twig
a warbler
wipes his muddy feet

Katatsumuri Soro-soronobore Fujinoyama

かたつむり そろそろ登れ 富士の山

Inch by inch—
Little snail
Creep up and up Mt. Fuji

Daikonbiki Daikonde Michi Oshiekeri

大根びき 大根で道おしえけり

The daikon picker
points the way
with his daikon

translations by Nanao Sakaki

KOBAYASHI ISSA (1763–1828) was born in Kashiwabara, Shinano, Japan, to a family of middle-class farmers. His pen name, Issa, means "one cup of tea," and he wrote over twenty thousand haikus in his lifetime, including fifty-four featuring snails.

The haiku has roots in the fifteenth century, when it was part of a tradition of linked verse, *renga.* According to contemporary Japanese usage, the haiku is an independent verse written in 5-7-5 syllables, and today eight to ten million people in Japan write haikus. In the United States, the haiku is also very popular, and, in schools, too much emphasis has probably been placed on the syllabic count as a method to write in this form.

I'd like to foreground the importance of a seasonal reference, *kigo,* in a haiku. The issue of transience, of a single moment, is fundamental, as is the haiku's immediacy, its present tense, its focus on deep noticing—these are all essential features that give strength to one of the world's shortest poetic forms. Also, there is some debate as to whether a haiku is best translated in three short phrases or in one continual motion. Hiroaki Sato points out that haikus in Japanese are printed in one continuous line, and he asserts that haikus translated into English are better rendered as such. For translating haikus into English, I suggest it's worth trying to make them in three lines and then in one line to see what works best.

My interest in Issa came through a personal connection with the poet and translator Nanao Sakaki. At one point, Nanao lived in Taos, New Mexico, and we once and only once had the pleasure of eating lunch together in Santa Fe. Nanao told me that during the Second World War he was a draftee in the Japanese navy and worked as a radar specialist. On the morning of August 6, 1945, he saw a single plane on his radar approach the coast of Japan. He looked outside and saw an enormous eruption in the sky and thought Mount Fuji had erupted. It turned out to be the atom bomb dropped on Hiroshima. I mention this incident because it was life-changing for Nanao. He became an itinerant poet and pursued a life of ecological consciousness; he also translated forty-five haikus by Issa into English. Over lunch, Nanao praised Issa's humility and humanity, and when I read Nanao's translations of Issa, I too became an admirer of Issa's work.

In the first haiku, I want to point out how Issa uses juxtaposition. Nanao chooses to translate Issa's haiku in three lines, and each line adds to what comes before to make one image. The opening image of the "blooming plum twig" embodies the *kigo,* the seasonal reference. The second line places a warbler on that twig, and the third line completes a juxtaposition, contrasting the beauty of the blooming plum twig with the muddy feet of the warbler.

Issa uses contrast of scale to empower the second haiku. The snail embodies the *kigo.* I'm not sure what month snails tend to emerge in Japan, but I take the little snail as a seasonal reference to spring. In spring, nature is emerging and flourishing, and Issa focuses attention on a little snail that creeps up and up—not a tree trunk or stone wall, but up Mount Fuji. Mount Fuji, which has spiritual weight in Japan, gives surprise and emotional power to the ending of this haiku. Some commentaries like to overlay an interpretation, where the snail can be seen as perseverance. In Spanish one might say, "Poco a poco se anda lejos," little by little one goes far. But to read this haiku in praise of perseverance is, I think, a disservice to the poem. The snail does what it does, it creeps along, and the context, the scale of creeping up Mount Fuji, is best experienced as part of a deep surprise.

I may have embellished Nanao's commentary, but I believe he told me over lunch that in the third haiku Issa is traveling and is looking for a village. Along the countryside road, Issa sees someone picking daikons, Japanese radishes, in a field. When Issa asks the way to this village, the daikon picker does not use words. Staying in sync with what he is doing, he pulls a daikon out of the earth and points the way, without stopping. In this fluid motion, the daikon picker not only gives directions to the village, he also follows the Tao 道 and shows how to live. In support of this reading, you can see in the kanji the Chinese character incorporated into the Japanese language: the character Tao 道 in the one line of Japanese; so, layering of meaning is another powerful technique employed in haikus to create depth and emotional power. When a particular word has meanings on two or more levels, it deepens the experience of the poem.

Interestingly, Nanao has chosen to use three lines in English for each of his Issa translations, and I suggest the three lines work well by accretion. In the third translation, he uses a dropped line to create a tiny moment of suspense before showing how the daikon picker "points the way." In all three translations, Nanao makes the foreign accessible, and the visual images become vehicles that move us emotionally and touch the universal.

ZONE 7

SAPPHO

Poem 31

φαίνεταί μοι κῆνος ἴσος θέοισιν
ἔμμεν᾽ ὤνηρ, ὄττις ἐνάντιός τοι
ἰσδάνει καὶ πλάσιον ἆδυ φωνεί-
          σας ὐπακούει

καὶ γελαίσας ἰμέροεν, τό μ᾽ ἦ μὰν
καρδίαν ἐν στήθεσιν ἐπτόαισεν·
ὠς γὰρ <ἔς> σ᾽ ἴδω βρόχε᾽ ὤς με φώνη-
          ς᾽ οὐδὲν ἔτ᾽ εἴκει,

ἀλλὰ καμ μὲν γλῶσσα ἔαγε, λέπτον
δ᾽ αὔτικα χρῶι πῦρ ὐπαδεδρόμακεν,
ὀππάτεσσι δ᾽ οὐδὲν ὄρημμ᾽, ἐπιβρό-
          μεισι δ᾽ ἄκουαι,

έκαδε μ᾽ ἴδρως κακχέεται, τρόμος δὲ
παῖσαν ἄγρει, χλωροτ⌊έρα δὲ π⌋οίας
ἔμμι, τεθ⌊νάκην δ᾽ ὀ⌋λίγω ᾽πιδε⌊ύης
          φα⌋ίνομ᾽ ἔμ᾽ αὔτ̣[αι.

ἀλλὰ πὰν τόλματον, ἐπεὶ καὶ πένητα

31

He seems to be a god, that man
Facing you, who leans to be close,
Smiles, and, alert and glad, listens
To your mellow voice

And quickens in love at your laughter
That stings my breasts, jolts my heart
If I dare the shock of a glance.
I cannot speak,

My tongue sticks to my dry mouth,
Thin fire spreads beneath my skin,
My eyes cannot see and my aching ears
Roar in their labyrinths.

Chill sweat slides down my body,
I shake, I turn greener than grass.
I am neither living nor dead and cry
From the narrow between.

But endure, even this grief of love.

translation by Guy Davenport

31

He seems to me equal to gods that man
whoever he is who opposite you
sits and listens close
        to your sweet speaking

and lovely laughing—oh it
puts the heart in my chest on wings
for when I look at you, even a moment, no speaking
        is left in me

no: tongue breaks and thin
fire is racing under skin
and in eyes no sight and drumming
        fills ears

and cold sweat holds me and shaking
grips me all, greener than grass
I am and dead—or almost
        I seem to me.

But all is to be dared, because even a person of poverty

translation by Anne Carson

31

He is more than a hero

He is a god in my eyes—
the man who is allowed
to sit beside you—he

who listens intimately
to the sweet murmur of
your voice, the enticing

laughter that makes my own
heart beat fast. If I meet
you suddenly, I can't

speak—my tongue is broken;
a thin flame runs under
my skin; seeing nothing,

hearing only my own ears
drumming, I drip with sweat;
trembling shakes my body

and I turn paler than
dry grass. At such times
death isn't far from me

translation by Mary Barnard

31

In my eyes he matches the gods, that man who
sits there facing you—any man whatever—
listening from closeby to the sweetness of your
        voice as you talk, the

sweetness of your laughter: yes, that—I swear it—
sets the heart to shaking inside my breast, since
once I look at you for a moment, I can't
        speak any longer,

but my tongue breaks down, and then all at once a
subtle fire races inside my skin, my
eyes can't see a thing and a whirring whistle
        thrums at my hearing,

cold sweat covers me and a trembling takes
ahold of me all over: I'm greener than the
grass is and appear to myself to be little
        short of dying.

But all must be endured, since even a poor [

translation by Jim Powell

SAPPHO (circa 620–550 BCE) came from an aristocratic family and lived on the island of Lesbos. Her poems are written in Aeolic Greek, a dialect spoken on that island. Almost all her poems are fragments written and edited on papyrus, but poem 31, also a fragment, has a major portion preserved because it was included in a treatise, *On the Sublime,* by Longinus (not to be mistaken for the later rhetorician Cassius Longinus). Longinus thinks of the sublime as a nobility of feeling through which we move beyond the human realm into an experience of mystery. In response to Sappho's poem, he turns to the reader and says, "Are you not astonished?" Sappho's 31 is one of her most famous poems, and I have included four outstanding translations, by Guy Davenport, Anne Carson, Mary Barnard, and Jim Powell, to discuss how these translators have used different resources of language to make the ancient contemporary.

In Guy Davenport's translation, you see right away how the fourth lines of the first four stanzas are shorter than the other lines of those stanzas. I do not read Greek, but as I understand it the three eleven-syllable lines of unrhymed quantitative verse (the "lesser Sapphic") are followed by one five-syllable line (the shorter "Adonic"), and this form, named the Sapphic stanza in the poet's honor, gives the poem its special rhythm and architecture. Davenport's opening is quick and effective. The triangular situation is immediately clear: The woman speaker is erotically charged as she sees another woman talking to a man. Davenport keeps his translation immediate, present tense, and the verbs are muscular. One-syllable verbs—"stings," "jolts," "sticks," and "roar"—are examples of how Davenport propels his translation forward. And a reader also notices right away that the poem is incomplete. The last one-line stanza, "But endure, even this grief of love," shows the poem goes on, but we've lost what happens beyond this tantalizing line.

In Anne Carson's translation, the fragmentary last line, "But all is to be dared, because even a person of poverty," is in stark contrast to Davenport's. Where Davenport uses "endure" to describe the situation, Carson turns it into a challenge, "all is to be dared." It's exciting to see how she enacts the inner experience of what is happening. Her interjection, "—oh it / puts the heart in my chest on wings," and then her repeated use of negation where "no speaking / is left in me // no:" enable the reader to experience firsthand the emotion of the speaker. Interestingly, in the third stanza, where Davenport intensifies the situation by personalizing—*my tongue, my mouth, my skin, my eyes, my ears*—Carson makes that stanza impersonal with *tongue, skin, eyes, ears.* This very different approach could be justified by arguing that, at this point in the poem, the speaker is so enflamed and chilled by emotion that, in her body, she can't claim her tongue, skin, eyes, and ears as belonging to her.

Mary Barnard's translation of Sappho, published in 1958, created a sensation for American readers. Before her, translations of Sappho were staid, and Mary Barnard found a way to make the poems come alive. I first read Sappho in Mary Barnard's translation, and it was thrilling to experience the immediacy of a contemporary voice. After all, these are poems written in Greek in the sixth century BCE, and I thought, what a gift these translations are! Barnard, unlike

Davenport and Carson, does not follow the Sapphic stanza. Instead, she radically reenvisions the form in tercets, and her enjambed lines create a flow of language, like water spilling and cascading downward. Barnard also opens with an arresting one-line stanza that leads into the tercets: "He is more than a hero // He is a god in my eyes—" That's a daring opening, and, of all the translations, I still prefer the delicacy of her phrasing with "a thin flame runs under / my skin," in contrast to "fire." Yet, the Barnard translation doesn't include the fragmentary last line and instead hints at incompletion by not ending with a period. Ending with "At such times / death isn't far from me" gives a temporary finality, whereas Davenport and Carson, by extending into "endure" or "dared," show that the poem is about to move into another direction and dimension.

In the fragmentary last line, Jim Powell echoes Davenport with the verb "endured," then he diverges from "grief of love" and aligns with Carson in "poor," but here he adds a single bracket opening to the right to visually startle a reader into seeing that something, or a lot, is missing. The single bracket is a wonderful visual feature Powell employs to heighten the sense of incompletion. He works effectively with sounds in English—"a whirring whistle / thrums at my hearing"—and his stanza-breaking and line-breaking after the words "the" and "a," so unexpected, are risky and daring. These line breaks create moments of hesitation and suspense that spill onto the next stanza or line.

As a poet who does not read Greek, I believe any reader, translator, or writer can learn from each of these translations. To see how a translation can be a source of inspiration and transformation for further writing, look at Catullus 51, where Catullus translates Sappho but then moves the poem in an entirely different direction in the final stanza. And, finally, because Sappho 31 is such a powerful, enduring poem that gathers and coalesces the most striking confluence of emotions, more translations, more transient worlds, will continue to be made.

ZONE 8

Sólo la muerte

Hay cementerios solos,
tumbas llenas de huesos sin sonido,
el corazón pasando un túnel
oscuro, oscuro, oscuro,
como un naufragio hacia adentro nos morimos,
como ahogarnos en el corazón,
como irnos cayendo desde la piel al alma.

Hay cadáveres,
hay pies de pegajosa losa fría,
hay la muerte en los huesos,
como un sonido puro,
como un ladrido sin perro,
saliendo de ciertas campanas, de ciertas tumbas,
creciendo en la humedad como el llanto o la lluvia.

Yo veo, solo, a veces,
ataúdes a vela
zarpar con difuntos pálidos, con mujeres de trenzas muertas,
con panaderos blancos como ángeles,
con niñas pensativas casadas con notarios,
ataúdes subiendo el río vertical de los muertos,
el río morado,

hacia arriba, con las velas hinchadas por el sonido de la muerte,
hinchadas por el sonido silencioso de la muerte.

A lo sonoro llega la muerte
como un zapato sin pie, como un traje sin hombre,
llega a golpear con un anillo sin piedras y sin dedo,
llega a gritar sin boca, sin lengua, sin garganta.
Sin embargo sus pasos suenan
y su vestido suena, callado, como un árbol.

Yo no sé, yo conozco poco, yo apenas veo,
pero creo que su canto tiene color de violetas húmedas,
de violetas acostumbradas a la tierra,
porque la cara de la muerte es verde,
y la mirada de la muerte es verde,
con la aguda humedad de una hoja de violeta
y su grave color de invierno exasperado.

Pero la muerte va también por el mundo vestida de escoba,
lame el suelo buscando difuntos,
la muerte está en la escoba,
es la lengua de la muerte buscando muertos,
es la aguja de la muerte buscando hilo.

La muerte está en los catres:
en los colchones lentos, en las frazadas negras
vive tendida, y de repente sopla:
sopla un sonido oscuro que hincha sábanas,

y hay camas navegando a un puerto
en donde está esperando, vestida de almirante.

Nothing but Death

There are cemeteries that are lonely,
graves full of bones that do not make a sound,
the heart moving through a tunnel,
in it darkness, darkness, darkness,
like a shipwreck we die going into ourselves,
as though we were drowning inside our hearts,
as though we lived falling out of the skin into the soul.

And there are corpses,
feet made of cold and sticky clay,
death is inside the bones,
like a barking where there are no dogs,
coming out from bells somewhere, from graves somewhere,
growing in the damp air like tears or rain.

Sometimes I see alone
coffins under sail,
embarking with the pale dead, with women that have dead hair,
with bakers who are as white as angels,
and pensive young girls married to notary publics,
caskets sailing up the vertical river of the dead,
the river of dark purple,
moving upstream with sails filled out by the sound of death,
filled by the sound of death which is silence.

Death arrives among all that sound
like a shoe with no foot in it, like a suit with no man in it,
comes and knocks, using a ring with no stone in it, with no finger
in it,
comes and shouts with no mouth, with no tongue, with no throat.
Nevertheless its steps can be heard
and its clothing makes a hushed sound, like a tree.

I'm not sure, I understand only a little, I can hardly see,
but it seems to me that its singing has the color of damp violets,
of violets that are at home in the earth,
because the face of death is green,
and the look death gives is green,
with the penetrating dampness of a violet leaf
and the somber color of embittered winter.

But death also goes through the world dressed as a broom,
lapping the floor, looking for dead bodies,
death is inside the broom,
the broom is the tongue of death looking for corpses,
it is the needle of death looking for thread.

Death is inside the folding cots:
it spends its life sleeping on the slow mattresses,
in the black blankets, and suddenly breathes out:
it blows out a mournful sound that swells the sheets,

and the beds go sailing toward a port
where death is waiting, dressed like an admiral.

translation by Robert Bly

Only Death

There are lone cemeteries,
tombs filled with soundless bones,
the heart passing through a tunnel
dark, dark, dark;
like a shipwreck we die inward,
like smothering in our hearts,
like slowly falling from our skin down to our soul.

There are corpses,
there are feet of sticky, cold gravestone,
there is death in the bones,
like a pure sound,
like a bark without a dog,
coming from certain bells, from certain tombs,
growing in the dampness like teardrops or raindrops.

I see alone, at times,
coffins with sails
weighing anchor with pale corpses, with dead-tressed women,
with bakers white as angels,
with pensive girls married to notaries,
coffins going up the vertical river of the dead,
the dark purple river,
upstream, with the sails swollen by the sound of death,
swollen by the silent sound of death.

To resonance comes death
like a shoe without a foot, like a suit without a man,
she comes to knock with a stoneless and fingerless ring,
she comes to shout without mouth, without tongue,
        without throat.
Yet her steps sound
and her dress sounds, silent, like a tree.

I know little, I am not well acquainted, I can scarcely see,
but I think that her song has the color of moist violets,
of violets accustomed to the earth,
because the face of death is green,
and the gaze of death is green,
with the sharp dampness of a violet leaf
and its dark color of exasperated winter.

But death also goes through the world dressed as a broom,
she licks the ground looking for corpses,
death is in the broom,
it is death's tongue looking for dead bodies,
it is death's needle looking for thread.

Death is in the cots:
in the slow mattresses, in the black blankets
she lives stretched out, and she suddenly blows:
she blows a dark sound that puffs out sheets,

and there are beds sailing to a port
where she is waiting, dressed as an admiral.

translation by Donald D. Walsh

NEFTALÍ RICARDO REYES BASOALTO, born in Chile in 1904, took the pen name Pablo Neruda in 1920 and legally changed his name in 1946. His first book of poetry, *Veinte poemas de amor y una canción desesperada* (*Twenty Love Poems and a Song of Despair*), published in 1924, received acclaim. Neruda was invited to join the foreign service and, from 1927 to 1944, he was appointed Chilean consul to Burma, Singapore, Java, India, Buenos Aires, Barcelona, Madrid, and eventually Mexico City. It was during the early years, deeply isolated and living in the Far East, that Pablo Neruda wrote the dark, surreal poems published in the first two volumes of *Residencia en la tierra* (*Residence on Earth*). Neruda went on to write poems in many different styles, from the political poems of *Canto general* (*Canto General*) to poems of praise in *Odas elementales* (*Elemental Odes*). He received the Nobel Prize in Literature in 1971 and died in 1973.

Pablo Neruda visited the US Library of Congress twice, first on March 5, 1943, and then on June 20, 1966. Neruda's first visit came at the invitation of Librarian of Congress Archibald MacLeish and Francisco Aguilera, assistant chief of the Hispanic Division; years later, in 1966, Francisco Aguilera recorded Neruda reading portions of *Alturas de Macchu Picchu* (*The Heights of Macchu Picchu*) for the Library of Congress's Archive of Hispanic Literature on Tape, now called the PALABRA Archive. When I visited the Library of Congress and met with Alyson Williams and Catalina Gómez (supervisory librarian and curator of the PALABRA Archive, respectively) in the Hispanic Reading Room, they played that recording of Pablo Neruda reading the opening passage to *Alturas de Macchu Picchu.* As I listened, I was surprised and thrilled to hear Neruda lean on his vowel-driven sounds to propel his poetry forward.

"Sólo la muerte" ("Nothing but Death") is one of my favorite Neruda poems, and it's from *Residencia en la tierra II.* The poem is arresting and full of startling images; death is everywhere, inescapable, and yet there's also a touch of dark humor with death waiting "dressed as an admiral." The sounds and rhythms—for example, "hay pies de pegajosa losa fría"—are memorable and compelling.

In looking at Robert Bly's and Donald Walsh's translations of Neruda's poem, it's clear right away that Walsh follows the Spanish very closely. The word "hay" in Spanish is so short and compressed that the translation in English of "there is" or "there are" feels wordy. Bly's opening line, "There are cemeteries that are lonely," feels a little verbose, whereas Walsh's "There are lone cemeteries" adheres more closely to the Spanish. In Neruda's fourth line, "oscuro, oscuro, oscuro," the repetition and vowel sounds are wonderful and have the effect of moving into darkness. Bly uses "darkness" three times, whereas Walsh repeats "dark." As I compare the two translations, it seems to me the Walsh is more accurate, literally closer to Neruda's Spanish, and yet the effect is disappointing. The phrase "there are feet of sticky, cold gravestone" feels flat, whereas Bly's "feet made of cold and sticky clay" is more animated. As the translations continue, Bly's poem gathers momentum in the third and fourth stanzas. The opening line to the fourth stanza, "Death arrives among all that sound," is superior to Walsh's "To resonance comes death." In Bly's translation, death is personified, active, and a force, whereas in Walsh's phrase, death strikes me as more passive, as more the receiver. Interestingly, as Bly continues with "death," Walsh picks up on Neruda's "la muerte" and translates death as "she": "she comes to knock" and "she comes to shout."

The opening line of the fifth stanza is "Yo no sé, yo conozco poco, yo apenas veo," which Bly translates as "I'm not sure, I understand only a little, I can hardly see," and is rendered by Walsh as "I know little, I am not well acquainted, I can scarcely see." I like Walsh's "I can scarcely see," but the two preceding phrases again strike me as sluggish. In the end, I recognize that Walsh understands the Spanish better than Bly, and maybe Bly has made some textual errors in his translation, but I believe comparing these two translations exemplifies the fact that literally following the source language is no guarantee of success. Neruda's poem is full of surprising twists, up to and including the final image of death "dressed like an admiral," and a good translation needs to enact these surprises. A translator needs to take imaginative risks and imbue the translation with emotional vitality. Simply in terms of rhythm, I respond to the momentum behind the voice in Bly's translation and find his more engaging.

ZONE 9

ANONYMOUS

Song of Songs 2:8–13

ק֣וֹל דּוֹדִ֔י הִנֵּה־זֶ֖ה בָּ֑א מְדַלֵּג֙ עַל־הֶ֣הָרִ֔ים מְקַפֵּ֖ץ עַל־הַגְּבָעֽוֹת׃
דּוֹמֶ֤ה דוֹדִי֙ לִצְבִ֔י א֖וֹ לְעֹ֣פֶר הָֽאַיָּלִ֑ים הִנֵּה־זֶ֤ה עוֹמֵד֙ אַחַ֣ר כָּתְלֵ֔נוּ מַשְׁגִּ֙יחַ֙
מִן־הַ֣חַלֹּנ֔וֹת מֵצִ֖יץ מִן־הַחֲרַכִּֽים׃
עָנָ֥ה דוֹדִ֖י וְאָ֣מַר לִ֑י ק֥וּמִי לָ֛ךְ רַעְיָתִ֥י יָפָתִ֖י וּלְכִי־לָֽךְ׃
כִּֽי־הִנֵּ֥ה הַסְּתָ֖ו עָבָ֑ר הַגֶּ֕שֶׁם חָלַ֖ף הָלַ֥ךְ לֽוֹ׃
הַנִּצָּנִים֙ נִרְא֣וּ בָאָ֔רֶץ עֵ֥ת הַזָּמִ֖יר הִגִּ֑יעַ וְק֥וֹל הַתּ֖וֹר נִשְׁמַ֥ע בְּאַרְצֵֽנוּ׃
הַתְּאֵנָה֙ חָֽנְטָ֣ה פַגֶּ֔יהָ וְהַגְּפָנִ֥ים ׀ סְמָדַ֖ר נָ֣תְנוּ רֵ֑יחַ ק֥וּמִי (לכי) [לָ֛ךְ] רַעְיָתִ֥י
יָפָתִ֖י וּלְכִי־לָֽךְ׃ {ס}

Song of Songs 2:8–13

The sound of my lover
coming from the hills
quickly, like a deer
upon the mountains

Now at my windows,
walking by the walls,
here at the lattices
he calls—

Come with me,
my love,
come away

For the long wet months are past,
the rains have fed the earth
and left it bright with blossoms

Birds wing in the low sky,
dove and songbird singing
in the open air above

Earth nourishing tree and vine,
green fig and tender grape,
green and tender fragrance

Come with me,
my love,
come away

translation by Marcia Falk

BÚFFALO CONDE

Xnich k'anal tak'in

Yawil yawal sts'unu/b te kajwal
ch'ul uch'oja/il yu/un jlekilal,
te ba-a xmaal te ta te/ tikil te ba ya xkux yo/tan te/tikil wakax
la/me ta jtojol namej k'inal kajwal.

Talon ta jk'inal, joy jmajtanat
te jtolja/ sok te ya/lel sit te/ak' kuch'ojix, joy jmajtanat,
uch'a bayel ya/yel sit te/ak' joy jmatanat
ja/ sk'op jmamalal te ya x-ik'awan.

Flor de oro

Fuente de huertos de mi amado,
noria de aguas sagradas para mi honor,
que corren del campo donde descansa el búfalo:
venga mi amado Legendario.

"Ya vine a mi campo, oh amada, compañera mía;
mi agua y mi jugo he bebido, esposa mía:
tomad abundante jugo, amada mía."
Es la voz de mi esposo que llama.

Flower of Gold

Fountain in the orchard of my beloved,
watermill sanctified in my honor,
that flows from the fields where the buffalo rests:
come here my legendary Beloved.

"I've come to my field, oh beloved, my companion;
I've drunk of my water and my juice, my wife:
now you should drink plentifully of this juice, my beloved."
It is the voice of my husband that calls.

translation by Michael Wiegers

BÚFFALO CONDE

Ta te/ak'etik yorail ya x-ajk'otajik

Ak'a-on jich bit'il marka-il ta wo/tan, jich bit'il senya-il ta k'a/b
bayel tolja/etik ma xtup' yu/un te sbujts' o/tanil,
kapaluk ma xtup' uch'oja/il ja/nix jich ma sjik'an te uk'um
ta sba lum k'inal sbujts' te jk'u/jpak'.

Te k'alal a kilbe te sit pajal sok te tolja/ ja/me ya/k'olal k'inal
jo/on pajk'on, te jchu' pajal sok t'ujbil ti'nel,
la xiwitesben jch'ulel te ajk'ubal,
te stotsil a jol pahal sok ipal ijk'al palomax.

Tiempo de bailar los árboles

Ponme como un sello sobre tu corazón, como una marca sobre
tu brazo.
Las muchas aguas no podrán apagar el amor,
ni lo ahogarán los ríos ni los pozos
sobre las montañas de los aromas de mi ropa.

Desde que fui en sus ojos como la que lleva alegría,
yo soy muro y mis pechos bonitas puertas;
por los sustos de la noche de mi alma,
tus cabellos como parvadas de palomas negras.

Time for Trees to Dance

Put me like a seal over your heart, like a mark on your arm.
All the waters will not extinguish love,
nor the rivers and springs drown it
over the mountains of scents in my clothes.

Ever since I went past your eyes as one filled with joy,
I am a wall and my breasts beautiful doors;
from the nightmares of my soul,
your hair is like a flock of black doves.

translation by Michael Wiegers

THE SONG OF SONGS, also known as the Song of Solomon, is the only book of love poems in the Bible. The poem narrates an intense love story between a woman and a man through a series of sensual dialogues and episodes. Although Christian and Jewish traditions have treated this work as religious allegory, the poem is essentially a celebration of human love. The Song of Songs is remarkable for its fresh language expressing female and male desire, for its emotional complexity, and for its expression of mutuality in a loving relationship. Some scholars date this work at around 300 BCE, and, with a text so old, the author is unknown. It's possible the texts, like Homer's works, involve a compilation over time. Both works show sources rooted in the oral tradition with repetition, refrain, and other musical features.

This work has been translated, interpreted, and arranged so many times over so many years that these cumulative translations of a single text are examples of transient worlds. It is included as the Song of Solomon in the King James Bible (1611), and here I've chosen Marcia Falk's translation published almost four hundred years later (2004). I have selected chapter 2, verses 8–13, and, in these verses, the passages in roman text are spoken by a woman, the passages in italics by a man. This passage opens with sound, "The sound of my lover / coming from the hills / quickly, like a deer / upon the mountains." Then the lover arrives: "at my windows . . . here at the lattices / he calls—" The man mentions "*Earth nourishing tree and vine,*" and with it is the implication that now is time for love:

"*Come with me, / my love, / come away.*"

Marcia Falk's translation is clear, supple, and moving for its immediacy. She describes her journey as a translator as that of a voyager moving closer, then farther away, then closer to the contours of the original poem. She does not get fixated on a single line or phrase but follows the arc of the poem, and she asserts that a translation begins by first finding its particular shape and voice; she adds that she hopes her translation will not only be read but read aloud. Then and only then a text over two thousand years old will come to life for people today.

It's a mystery and a marvel to think how a poem as old as the Song of Songs, translated so many times, into so many languages, can find its way across the world. Búffalo Conde is the magical pseudonym of the poet Pedro Pérez Conde, who is from Tenejapa, Chiapas, Mexico, and whose Mayan culture has a long history of animism and shamanism. When Pérez Conde uses the name Búffalo Conde, he is invoking the tradition of magical realism, where every day unexpected, miraculous things happen. And as a poet-translator he also suggests that he is an outsider—buffalo are not native to Chiapas—and an intermediary for the worlds of spirits and beliefs, as well as between languages.

In Búffalo Conde's "Flower of Gold" and "Time for Trees to Dance," a reader immediately notices how the spontaneity and fresh, mythic language have deep roots in the Song of Songs. Here roman text is used for a woman speaker, and a man's words are placed inside quotation marks. In the Song of Songs, a beloved's eyes may be compared to a flock of doves, but Búffalo Conde—maybe there's a touch of surrealism here—writes, “from the nightmares of my soul, / your hair is like a flock of black doves.” And, more important than any specific image or set of images that have carried over across millennia, Conde’s song has a spiritual core where the liberated eros of romantic love is celebrated and is sacred.

If one thinks of languages as living roots and branches, a poem with a Hebrew root can travel up into Spanish and then out into a Mayan leaf. Given the long history of Christian colonization in Mexico, Michael Wiegers says he assumes that Búffalo Conde wrote or read these poems in Spanish then translated them into Tzeltal; and Búffalo Conde’s poems could pass for the language of the Song of Solomon in the King James Bible. Catholicism (which in turn has been influenced by Judaism) arrived in Mexico initially from Spain, whose language is itself heavily influenced by Arabic-speaking Muslims. Lines of authenticity and originality become blurred, and translation becomes a subversive act that undercuts colonial borders and highlights the blend of cultures as language and poetry move across and transcend them. Translation can be a daily, ordinary act of movement from one language into another as one human being seeks understanding and connection, and it can also be a vehicle to dissolve boundaries. Here the mystery and magic of Búffalo Conde is that his poems flow across space and time: The voices of female and male desire in his poems are intimately connected to those in the Song of Songs.

ZONE 10

MARINA TSVETAEVA

Мне нравится, что Вы больны не мной

Мне нравится, что Вы больны не мной,
Мне нравится, что я больна не Вами,
Что никогда тяжёлый шар земной
Не уплывёт под нашими ногами.
Мне нравится, что можно быть смешной—
Распущенной—и не играть словами,
И не краснеть удушливой волной,
Слегка соприкоснувшись рукавами.

Мне нравится ещё, что Вы при мне
Спокойно обнимаете другую,
Не прочите мне в адовом огне
Гореть за то, что я не Вас целую.
Что имя нежное моё, мой нежный, не
Упоминаете ни днём, ни ночью—всуе . . .
Что никогда в церковной тишине
Не пропоют над нами: аллилуйя!

Спасибо Вам и сердцем и рукой
За то, что Вы меня—не зная сами!—
Так любите: за мой ночной покой,
За редкость встреч закатными часами,

За наши не-гулянья под луной,
За солнце не у нас над головами,
За то, что Вы больны—увы!—не мной,
За то, что я больна—увы!—не Вами!

I'm glad your sickness

I'm glad your sickness is not caused by me.
Mine is not caused by you. I'm glad to know
the heavy earth will never flow away
from us, beneath our feet, and so
we can relax together, and not watch
our words. When our sleeves touch
we shall not drown in waves of rising blush.

I'm glad to see you calmly now embrace
another girl in front of me, without
any wish to cause me pain, as you
don't burn if I kiss someone else.
I know you never use my tender name,
my tender spirit, day or night. And
no one in the silence of a church
will sing their Hallelujahs over us.

Thank you for loving me like this,
for you feel love, although you do not know it.
Thank you for the nights I've spent in quiet.
Thank you for the walks under the moon
you've spared me and those sunset meetings unshared.
Thank you. The sun will never bless our heads.

Take my sad thanks for this: you do not cause
my sickness. And I don't cause yours.

translation by Elaine Feinstein

I like that it's not me

I like that it's not me you pine for,
And like that I don't pine for you,
That we stand on solid ground
And will never get swept away.
Maybe I like playing fast and loose,
To be wordlessly suggestive,
But no heat lightning annihilates me
When our wrists glance.

I don't mind that right in front of me
You take someone else in your arms;
I'm glad you don't curse me out
Just because it's not you I kiss.
No endearing nickname, my dearest,
Do you call me day and night—in vain . . .
And never, under an altar's hush,
Will blessings ring our head: Hallelujah!

Hand over heart, I thank you:
That you—without giving it a thought!—
Love me this way: that my nights are quiet,
That we don't promenade at sunset
Or rendezvous under the full moon,
That the sun doesn't shine as if just for us,

That you deny—any?—longing for me
While I deny—also—longing for you.

translation by Carol Moldaw

MARINA TSVETAEVA (1892–1941) was born in Moscow. In 1912, she married poet Sergei Efron, and they had two daughters and later one son. During years of famine after the Russian Revolution, she had to place her daughters in a state orphanage. In 1922, she immigrated with her family to Berlin, then Prague, and, in 1925, settled in Paris. Sergei Efron was recruited by and worked for the Soviet secret police, and Tsvetaeva was ostracized by the Russian expatriate community. In 1939, Tsvetaeva returned to the Soviet Union, and her husband was executed. When the German army invaded the Soviet Union, she and her son evacuated to Yelabuga. On August 31, 1941, suffering from hunger and despair, she hanged herself.

Marina Tsvetaeva is one of the modern masters of Russian poetry, and her poems, characterized by swift shifts of focus and unusual syntax, are particularly difficult to translate. Her ruling passion during her life was poetry: She said that if she were offered a chance to go beyond the ocean into paradise but were forbidden to write, she would reject paradise.

"I'm glad your sickness" is an early lyrical poem by Marina Tsvetaeva, and this zone shows how even if you don't know a second language, you can turn to someone fluent in it and create your own moving translation. Carol Moldaw has a friend, Irina Ross, who grew up in Russia and left at age twenty-five. Ross loves Russian poetry and knows poems by heart, and Moldaw, who for decades has known many Russian poems in translation, did not want to be influenced by rereading translations, so she asked Ross to choose poems for her to translate. Ross chose one by Osip Mandelstam, another by Anna Akhmatova, and a third by Marina Tsvetaeva. I've chosen the last one to discuss with Elaine Feinstein's translation, but, before I do, I want to share how Carol Moldaw made her translation.

Moldaw said she started by recording Ross reading the poem in Russian, so she could hear the sounds whenever she wanted. Ross provided a transliteration of the Cyrillic poem as well as a crib. Moldaw typed out the transliteration and printed it in blue ink; underneath the transliteration, she typed and printed out the words of Ross's crib in red ink, and then, underneath, she hand-wrote English words in pencil. Eventually she typed her English under Ross's crib, so she had three lines, color coded, to refer to each line of the poem in Cyrillic. Moldaw went over the transliterations and looked for assonance, rhyme, half-rhyme, parallel construction, and repetition. She decided not to try to duplicate the Russian rhymes but, instead, to use rich sounds in English where she heard rich sounds in Russian. She also looked for equivalent gestures, not too slangy or colloquial, that read naturally in English and imparted the power she felt in the original.

Moldaw looked word by word, line by line at the Russian but was not strapped to it. For instance, in line 7, she had the Russian transliteration "I ne krasnet udushlivoy volnoi" in blue ink and Ross's crib "And not blush with a stifling wave" in red ink. Moldaw thought about how to render that into English, and she came up with, "But no heat lightning annihilates me."

Moldaw's English translation of Marina Tsvetaeva's poem follows the architecture of three eight-line stanzas, and her lines 4 to 8 move freely:

> Maybe I like playing fast and loose,
> To be wordlessly suggestive,
> But no heat lightning annihilates me
> When our wrists glance.

Interestingly, Elaine Feinstein, instead of making three eight-line stanzas, has stanzas of seven lines, eight lines, and eight lines. Her translation opens strongly with "I'm glad your sickness is not caused by me." Then she condenses Russian lines 4 to 8 into three lines of English:

> we can relax together, and not watch
> our words. When our sleeves touch
> we shall not drown in waves of rising blush.

Feinstein goes for the sound at the end of the lines, with "watch," "touch," and "blush." Moldaw invents "heat lightning" and personifies "wrists" to translate the experience.

Feinstein translates the last two lines of the second stanza as:

> no one in the silence of a church
> will sing their Hallelujahs over us.

Her lines are direct and make a statement, whereas Moldaw activates

"Hallelujah" and uses sound, and silence, in a different way:

> And never, under an altar's hush,
> Will blessings ring our head: Hallelujah!

Feinstein translates the poem's closing lines as:

> Take my sad thanks for this: you do not cause
> my sickness. And I don't cause yours.

This phrasing feels flat to me. Moldaw looked at the transliteration and saw that *uvy!,* "alas," is repeated in Russian. Ross's crib has "For you, not longing—alas—for me," and in the last line "For me not longing—alas—for you." Moldaw liked the repetitions and decided to keep the dashes, but she thought "alas" was too dated to use in English. She replaced the "alas" with "any" and "also," added a touch of doubt by making "any" a question, then set those words off by dashes. Her ending enacts a contrast:

> That you deny—any?—longing for me
> While I deny—also—longing for you.

It's clear a memorable translation can be made even if you don't know the language the poem is written in. You will need to find someone fluent in the language who can collaborate closely with you, and it's important you care about, better yet, love the poem you translate. Translation involves building bridges, and here it can be between people. I suggest you reach out to a family member, a teacher, or a friend and try translating a poem from a language you do not know.

ZONE 11

AIMÉ CÉSAIRE

mot-macumba

le mot est père des saints
le mot est mère des saints
avec le mot *coüresse* on peut traverser un fleuve peuplé de caïmans
il m'arrive de dessiner un mot sur le sol
avec un mot frais on peut traverser le désert
d'une journée
il y a des mots bâton-de-nage pour écarter les squales
il y a des mots iguanes
il y a des mots subtils ce sont des mots phasmes
il y a des mots d'ombre avec des réveils en colère d'étincelles
il y a des mots Shango
il m'arrive de nager de ruse sur le dos d'un mot dauphin

Macumba Word

the word is the father of the saints
the word is the mother of the saints
with the word *couresse* one can cross a river swarming with caimans
sometimes i trace a word in the dirt
with a fresh word one can cross the desert in a single day
there are swim-stick words for pushing away sharks
there are iguana words
there are subtle words those are stick-insect words
there are shadow words that awake sparking with anger
there are Shango words
sometimes i even sneak a swim on the back of a dolphin word

translation by Clayton Eshleman
and Annette Smith

NOTES

macumba: an African (Bantu) word referring to magic

couresse: a grass snake of Martinique

Shango: Yoruba god associated with fire, lightning, and thunder

caiman: a species of crocodile

dolphin: "dauphin" in French, the heir apparent to France's throne, also an Amazon river dolphin of Afro-Brazilian religion

AIMÉ CÉSAIRE (1913–2008) was born in Basse-Pointe in Martinique. He went to France to study at the Parisian schools École Normale Supérieure and Lycée Louis-le-Grand, and there he met up with Senegalese poet Léopold Sédar Senghor. Together they created a journal, *L'Étudiant noir* (*Black Student*), that brought together student writers from Africa and the West Indies. Césaire first used the term *négritude* in the 1939 journal version of his landmark book-length poem, *Notebook of a Return to the Native Land.* Negritude as a movement was an embrace of Black identity and African culture, and it turned away from Europe to resist assimilation and the politics of colonialism. Césaire asserted "our heritage is one of fevers," and his poetry brought together a singular confluence of African myth and French Surrealism. He was also a playwright, was active in politics, and served as deputy to the French National Assembly. He died in Martinique at the age of ninety-four.

Sometimes writers issue manifestos to articulate a new group of aesthetic priorities. In 1924, André Breton issued a "Manifesto of Surrealism," in which he said that in honor of Guillaume Apollinaire, he was launching Surrealism as a movement where "psychic automatism" could have free reign. In this way, Surrealism drew on dream language rather than having the writer control a poem through some form of reason.

Aimé Césaire drew on principles of Surrealism, but he made a poetry entirely his own. His "Macumba Word" is a mini-manifesto that asserts the power of language and draws its inspiration from

Africa. The poem is a list, a naming, a small incantation, a spell. It asserts the raw and surprising power of language—"with a fresh word one can cross the desert in a single day"—and it raises issues of translation we haven't yet considered. Do a writer's ideas and beliefs become "translated" into the action of a poem? If "Macumba Word" brings forward the elemental power and magical efficacy of language, how is that power put into action? When the images of a poem do not follow a linear logic, do they need to be "translated" into some form of meaning?

As translators from French to English, Clayton Eshleman and Annette Smith have followed Césaire's French closely, and they have also judiciously borrowed a word from French when needed. The third line carries *couresse* into English, miming the action of one who crosses dangerous waters and arrives at dry land, and the action of the Anglophone reader who navigates the space between the original context of the word and its English-language network of sounds and associations (such as *course* and *chorus*). Without punctuation, phrases slip into phrases. One can argue that Césaire demolishes hierarchy in syntax and in image as each utterance flows into another.

The next line, "sometimes i trace a word in the dirt," does much to ground us. Importantly, Eshleman and Smith chose *trace* in place of the more direct translation *draw*. Their choice underscores that the source of the speaker's own word precedes him, is beyond him. This line along with the final line of the poem shows the speaker engaging directly with the natural world in an attitude of play. In the sequence of assertions, Césaire reveals the poem as a field of energy that affirms the power, efficacy, and even secrecy at the heart of language. The speaker follows wherever the word leads, and this spirit of play is at the core of Césaire's vision translated into poetry.

ZONE 12

NAJWAN DARWISH

ولَمْ نَكُن نَتَو قَّف

لَيسَ لي بَلَدٌ لأَرجِعَ إليها
لَيسَ لي بَلَدٌ لأُنفى مِنْها
شَجَرَةٌ جُذورُها ماءُ نَهرٍ يَجري
إنْ توقَّفَتْ تَموت
وإنْ لَمْ تَتَوقَّف تَموت.

***

على خَدِّ المَوت وعلى ذِراعِ المَوت
قَضَيْتُ أَفضَلَ أَيّامي
وبَلَدي التي خَسِرتُها كُلَّ يَومٍ
كُنتُ أَربَحُها كُلَّ يومٍ
وكان للنّاسِ بَلَدٌ واحِدةٌ
وكانت بَلَدي تَتَعَدَّدُ في الخَسارةِ
وتَتَجَدَّدُ في الفَقْدِ
ومِثْلي جُذورُها في المَاء
إنْ توقَّفتْ تَجِف
إنْ توقَّفتْ تموت
وكِلانا كانَ يَجري مع نَهرٍ مِنْ شُعاعِ الشَّمس
مِنْ غُبارِ الذَّهَبِ المُصّاعِدِ مِنْ جِراحٍ أَثَريَّةٍ
ولَمْ نَكُنْ نتوقَّفُ
كِلانا كانَ يَجري
لَمْ نُفكِّر مَرَّةً أَنْ نَتَوَقَّفَ لِنَلْتقي.

***

لَيسَ لي بَلَدٌ لأُنفى مِنْها
لَيسَ لي بَلَدٌ لأَرجِع إِلَيها
وإِنْ توقَّفتُ في بَلَدٍ أَموت.

We Never Stop

I have no country to return to,
no country to be banished from,
a tree whose roots
are a running river:
It dies if it stops,
it dies if it doesn't.

On the cheeks and arms of death
I spent the best of my days,
and the land I lost each day
I gained each day anew.
The people had a single country,
but mine multiplied in loss,
renewed itself in absence.
Its roots, like mine, are water:
If it stops it withers,
if it stops it dies.
Both of us are running
with a river of sunbeams,
a river of gold dust
that rises from ancient wounds,
and we never stop.
We keep on,
never thinking to pause
so our two paths can meet.

I have no country to be banished from,
no country to return to:
I'll die if I stop,
I'll die if I keep going.

translation by Kareem James Abu-Zeid

NAJWAN DARWISH was born in Jerusalem in 1978, and he lives in Haifa and Jerusalem. He is the author of nine books of poetry, and in English his books *Nothing More to Lose* (New York Review of Books, 2014), *Exhausted on the Cross* (NYRB, 2021), and *No One Will Know You Tomorrow: Selected Poems 2014–2024* (Yale University Press, 2024) are all translated by Kareem James Abu-Zeid. Darwish has been active in cultural journalism by cofounding independent magazines and newspapers. From 2006 to 2012, he worked as a cultural critic for the Lebanese newspaper *Al-Akhbar,* and he has also been an organizer and advisor to the Palestine Festival of Literature. Since 2014, he has been the chief cultural editor of the Arabic-language London-based newspaper *Al-Araby al-Jadeed* (*The New Arab*).

In "We Never Stop" (2014/2015) the speaker's perspective is that of an exile. The poem was written during a period of about seven months when Darwish's journalism work based him in London (the collection was published in Arabic in 2018). Many of the poems written then deal with exile as a Palestinian, and it's important to acknowledge the complexity of being Palestinian, in that the population of this diaspora around the world (Europe, North and South America, as well as the Middle East) is roughly the same as the number of Palestinians living within Palestine itself. Darwish usually resides within Palestine, but here he's writing from the perspective of being outside of it. Expulsion, exodus, diaspora—all of these are part and parcel of Palestinian identity now.

One of the remarkable things about this poem is how it transcends the context that it was written in. There are no specific acts of bloodshed, but the speaker of the poem and the country are always in tension, always running, and never able to even think of pausing "so our two paths can meet." The speaker starts, in the first two lines, with expulsion and exile: "I have no country to return to, / no country to be banished from," and the tension, the urgency, and the doom are articulated in "It dies if it stops, / it dies if it doesn't." The land, a feminine noun in Arabic, is often treated as a beloved, but here, it is "On the cheeks and arms of death / I spent the best of my days." The speaker, almost an archetypal speaker, recognizes "a single country . . . multiplied in loss," and he also recognizes a rich tradition of literature and culture from the ancient world in the images of "river of sunbeams" and "river of gold dust." A powerful moment for me is in the simple "If it stops it withers, / if it stops it dies." Both lines are about stopping, and I imagine the unstated contrast is "if it runs, it has a chance to live." And so the "I" and the country run and are endlessly running.

Kareem James Abu-Zeid translates from French and German as well as Arabic, and he says that "Arabic and English are so different that it's impossible to come up with anything like a word-for-word translation. You have to step back and reformulate everything, think about the syntax that works best, and be very careful to think on the level of image and also context. Arabic words have a very broad semantic range, as opposed to the relative specificity of English, so it's important to pay close attention to which semantic aspect of a given Arabic word best fits the poetic context." He adds that he pays a lot of attention to the sounds and rhythms of both the Arabic and the English and that in this poem, there's a quickness of rhythm, like a flowing river, a kind of breathlessness that comes from constant motion.

I'm impressed with the humanity in this poem and how the clarity does not exclude any underlying complexity. The speaker could easily launch into a bitter, polemical attack about the tragic state of affairs; instead, the poem transcends any bitterness, and the speaker connects to something larger than himself, not just the land and people of Palestine but also the rich poetic traditions of the Arabic language and indeed of other languages and cultures. Maybe it's Najwan Darwish's engagement with poetry that has saved him from falling into the trap of bitterness, or, as he once said, "I turned rebellion into poetry; rebellion turned me into a poet."

ZONE 13

INGER CHRISTENSEN

from *alfabet*

1

abrikostræerne findes, abrikostræerne findes

2

bregnerne findes; og brombær, brombær
og brom findes; og brinten, brinten

3

cikaderne findes; cikorie, chrom
og citrontræer findes; cikaderne findes;
cikaderne, ceder, cypres, cerebellum

4

duerne findes; drømmerne, dukkerne
dræberne findes; duerne, duerne;
dis, dioxin og dagene; dagene
findes; dagene døden; og digtene
findes; digtene, dagene, døden

5

efteråret findes; eftersmagen og eftertanken
findes; og enrummet findes; englene,
enkerne og elsdyret findes; enkelthederne
findes, erindringen, erindringens lys;
og efterlyset findes, egetræet og elmetræet
findes, og enebærbusken, ensheden, ensomheden
findes, og edderfuglen og edderkoppen findes,
og eddiken findes, og eftertiden, eftertiden

from *alphabet*

1

apricot trees exist, apricot trees exist

2

bracken exists; and blackberries, blackberries;
bromine exists; and hydrogen, hydrogen

3

cicadas exist; chicory, chromium,
citrus trees; cicadas exist;
cicadas, cedars, cypresses, the cerebellum

4

doves exist, dreamers, and dolls;
killers exist, and doves, and doves;
haze, dioxin, and days; days
exist, days and death; and poems
exist; poems, days, death

5

early fall exists; aftertaste, afterthought;
seclusion and angels exist;
widows and elk exist; every
detail exists; memory, memory's light;
afterglow exists; oaks, elms,
junipers, sameness, loneliness exist;
eider ducks, spiders, and vinegar
exist, and the future, the future

translation by Susanna Nied

INGER CHRISTENSEN (1935–2009) was born in Vejle, Denmark, and lived most of her life in Copenhagen. She spoke four languages, wrote poetry, fiction, drama, children's books, and essays, and drew on a wide range of interests—music, mathematics, fine art, science, and natural history—for her poetry. There was considerable lag time between the publications of her poetry books in Denmark and their translations into English and publication in the United States. *alphabet,* a book-length poem, was first published in Denmark in 1981 and then published in the United States in 2001. Her earlier book of poetry, *It,* published in Denmark in 1969, was not published in the United States until 2006. In the burgeoning global movement of ecopoetry, Inger Christensen's work is foundational. She was deeply shaken by environmental destruction (Hiroshima and Chernobyl, to cite just two examples) and the possibility that the earth cannot recover from what humans are doing, but she did not lose faith in recovery or in poetry.

Inger Christensen had a very special relationship with her translator Susanna Nied. Nied is the sole translator of Christensen's poetic works into English, and in that regard holds a unique position as an advocate for Christensen's poetry. In this zone, we can consider translation as lifelong collaboration based on mutual trust. In an interview, Nied talks about how she worked with Inger Christensen. In Copenhagen, Christensen would read a page of her poetry aloud in Danish, and Nied would read a page of her translation in English; they would then share comments and think about revisions and how to improve the English translation. Nied says she made revisions with close attention to the tonal shifts she heard when Christensen read aloud. Contradicting assumptions that translating from one language to another results in an immediate loss of the sounds of the original, Nied and Christensen's intimate collaboration over decades yields a translated poetry with the keenest attention to sound, rhythm, and musicality.

I've chosen the opening five stanzas to *alphabet.* This long poem uses two structures to shape its unfolding arc. The first is the Fibonacci sequence, in which each number is the sum of the previous two: 0, 1, 1, 2, 3, 5, 8, 13, 21, 34, 55, and so on. These numbers determine the number of lines to each stanza; also, the poem starts each stanza with a different letter of the alphabet, in order. By the time the poem arrives at the letter *n* (in mathematics, *n* is often used as the symbol for any number), the stanza has so many lines that the poem ends without formal closure. I mention these two structures to show not only how the poem is organized but also that there is no inherently unpoetic material. A poet can use anything. A poet needs imagination, emotion, and mastery of language; and look at how this translation unfolds in its first five stanzas.

The opening line, starting with *a,* with apricots, contains repetition: "apricot trees exist, apricot trees exist." The verb *exist* is the only verb running through the opening stanzas, and it makes a reader experience not only the miracle of what exists but also the underlying threat of nonexistence. With the second stanza,

bracken exists; and blackberries, blackberries;
bromine exists; and hydrogen, hydrogen

nature and chemical elements are brought into unstated tension and coexistence. Bromine and hydrogen are fundamental elements. Bromine exists in seawater compounds, and much of the loss of ozone in the earth's atmosphere above Antarctica is due to chemical reactions involving bromine. Yet Christensen never mentions these facts. She's writing a lyrical poem that begins with a single line and that opens and keeps opening up.

In nature, the arrangement of seed heads on sunflowers often follows the Fibonacci sequence. Often but not always. So there's a sense of how precarious and precious existence is. In stanza 4, the introduction of the word "killers" is a shock, and it's a shock that is immediate through sound; most of the stanza involves words that start with the letter *d.* "Killers" is sonically and thematically a shock; and again Christensen avoids any overt political stance. The poem will go on for over two hundred lines and include a factual description of people killed in the atomic blast over Hiroshima before the speaker finally emerges with "I stand in / my kitchen peeling / potatoes."

When I first read *alphabet,* I was thrilled and couldn't put it down. I've come back to it many times, and I am still thrilled at how musical, moving, and alive this poem is in English. What a gift Susanna Nied has provided through collaborative translation.

ZONE 14

Song one

गोहने गुपाल फिरूँ, ऐसी आवत मण में ॥टेक॥
अवलोकत वारिज बदन बिबस भई तण में।
मुरली कर लकुट लेऊँ, पीत बसन धारूँ।
काछा गोप भेष मुगुट, गोधन संग चारूँ।
हम भई गुलफाम लता, बृन्दावन रैनाँ।
पशु पंछी मरकट मुना श्रवण सुणत बैनाँ।
गुरूजन कठिन कानि कासों री कहिए।
मीराँ प्रभु गिरधर मिलि ऐसे ही रहिए ॥

Mira Wears God's Clothes

I thought, what if I went around dressed up as him?

When I see his face blooming, willpower deserts me—

what if I went

Could I take up his flute and staff, put on his yellow robe?
Wear his herder's clothes and crown? Take the cattle out to graze?

disguised

Or else become a vine, growing from the soil in his village?
With the birds and monkeys, and the sages deep in conversation?

couldn't I?

My teachers, it's so hard to be conventional! How to even explain?
Mira says, what if I met with my mountain-lifting Lord

and stayed just like that, with him?

translation by Chloe Martinez

Song two

या ब्रज में कछू देख्यो री टोना ॥टेक॥
ले मटुकी सिर चली गुजरिया, आगे मिले बाबा नंदजी के छौना।
दधि को नाम बिसरि गयी प्यारी, 'लेबहु री कोई श्याम सलोना'।
वृन्दावन की कुंज गलिन में, आँख लगाइ गयो मनमोहना।
मीराँ के प्रभु गिरधर नागर, सुन्दर स्याम सुघर सलोना ॥

Mira Tells a Story

In Braj Village I witnessed something wild:

a milkmaid put her pitcher on her head, and saw

God.

She forgot the word "yogurt."
She called out the Beloved's name instead:

"Come and get some tasty Krishna!"

In the groves and lanes of the village, the Mesmerizer
draws
every
eye.

Mira's man is Lord Mountain-Lifter:

The Dark One.
The Dreamy.
The Delectable.

translation by Chloe Martinez

MIRABAI (1498–1546) was a renowned mystic poet who lived in northern India. She was a Rajput princess who became a devotee of Krishna very early in her life, and she married into a Rajput royal family in the Marwar region of Rajasthan. Her songs to Krishna invoke a woman's passion for her beloved, addressing Krishna as a cowherd, a flute player, and even as The Dark One. As a poet she is known as an independent woman whose devotion is entangled with desire and who stands up for what is right.

As the guest editor of *Best Literary Translations* (Deep Vellum, 2026), I was excited to read Chloe Martinez's translations of Mirabai's poetry. When I looked at the poems in Braj Bhasha and then at the translations, I felt that Martinez found a way to "unpack" the poems into contemporary English. I was impressed with how clear and spontaneous Mirabai's voice was, and I liked how Martinez used the space of the page to give the translations shape. For this zone, I interviewed Chloe Martinez.

ARTHUR SZE: I of course can't read Mirabai in the original, but as I look at the text and your translations, it seems to me you've unpacked and loosened them to fit into contemporary speech. Was your process of translation like this or something very different?

CHLOE MARTINEZ: When I first began translating these poems, I was bound and determined (like every newbie translator, probably) to make them look like faithful copies of the original texts, with the same lineation and minimal added syntax and punctuation, even trying to hew as close as possible to word/phrase order, though I didn't go so far as to attempt to copy the rhymes (most of these poems use rhymed couplets, and some use the same end rhyme throughout—that's just a *painful* amount of rhyming in English). It seemed hard, the results seemed not great, but I thought, that's how you're supposed to do it! Then I stopped translating Mira for many years (LIFE), but I kept on reading about her, listening to sung versions of the poems, and reading other South Asian poetry in translation (Mani Rao's brilliant Bhagavad Gita translation, for example). When I came back to translating Mira, it seemed obvious (how did I miss it before??) that preserving the look of a poem on the page might not *always* be the best way to honor its music, or to invite a reader into its world. So I started again, letting my translations breathe a bit this time. I was still trying to keep the meaning of each line intact—the couplet as a discrete unit of meaning is an important formal constraint in the originals—but I started to let the spacing in and around the lines be more free, creating little pockets of emphasis or breath. I began to see my job as less like a Xerox machine, more like a singer interpreting a song.

I also let more contemporary language come in, which felt transgressive at first, but gradually has come to feel like the opposite. Mira's speech is sometimes pretty close to colloquial for her time; she was also writing in a vernacular (i.e., not Persian or Sanskrit). Furthermore, the intimacy with which she's speaking to God is a central feature of the poems, and I think a little colloquial/contemporary speech helps bring us into that intimate space with her.

AS: What were the most exciting and challenging aspects of translating Mirabai?

CM: One important aspect of the poems that I wrestled with for a while was the refrain. In most printed versions of these poems there is a refrain notation after the first line (sometimes the first two lines); singers tend to repeat that refrain after every one to two couplets of the poem, often drawing it out meditatively. The single line thus takes on extra meanings in dialogue with the couplets. Most translators don't address this dimension of the poems, but I started feeling that I had to deal with it somehow. I experimented with just repeating the refrain throughout the translation, but that felt like too much repetition on the page. The approach I settled on is to repeat fragments and/or alternate translations of the refrain, as I do in "Mira Wears God's Clothes." That feels to me like the sung effect, in which you hear new emphases and ideas each time the refrain recurs. Figuring out that there could be a way to convey this in a translation was exciting and satisfying for me. It's also so delicious, as a translator, to let that one line be a place of multiplicity and process—to show the reader a few versions, with their different charms. ("Mira Tells a Story" is a rare instance in which I didn't do this. The storytelling aspect of that poem, and the fact that Mira is the witness to most of the poem's action, might have something to do with this. The repeated refrain felt, even in fragments, a bit intrusive to me for that poem.)

AS: Is there anything you want to say about background or anything else you want to say about these two poems?

CM: I guess one more thing I'd say is that these are religious poems—Mira is often portrayed as a docile, white-clad saint figure—but they're also a bit subversive. A woman claiming authority (not to mention claiming God as her own) to the degree that Mira does was more than a little radical in her time, and still feels that way to me. In a poem like "Mira Wears God's Clothes," for example, Mira describes Krishna's presence as overpowering, then proposes that she can be with him with a kind of intensity and permanence that she can't even explain—but that feels convincing all the same. In "Mira Tells a Story," too, she is describing being entranced, but she is also the one entrancing us. I think that doubling of submission and empowerment is very Mira, and is one of the things that aligns her for me with someone like Dickinson. Both poets have a gift for showing us a flower in one hand, the cosmos in the other.

ZONE 15

RAINER MARIA RILKE

Archaïscher Torso Apollos

Wir kannten nicht sein unerhörtes Haupt,
darin die Augenäpfel reiften. Aber
sein Torso glüht noch wie ein Kandelaber,
in dem sein Schauen, nur zurückgeschraubt,

sich hält und glänzt. Sonst könnte nicht der Bug
der Brust dich blenden, und im leisen Drehen
der Lenden könnte nicht ein Lächeln gehen
zu jener Mitte, die die Zeugung trug.

Sonst stünde dieser Stein entstellt und kurz
unter der Schultern durchsichtigem Sturz
und flimmerte nicht so wie Raubtierfelle;

und bräche nicht aus allen seinen Rändern
aus wie ein Stern: denn da ist keine Stelle,
die dich nicht sieht. Du mußt dein Leben ändern.

Archaic Torso of Apollo

We did not know his legendary head,
in which the eyeballs ripened. But
his torso still glows like a candelabrum
in which his gaze, only turned low,

holds and gleams. Else could not the curve
of the breast blind you, nor in the slight turn
of the loins could a smile be running
to that middle, which carried procreation.

Else would this stone be standing maimed and short
under the shoulders' translucent plunge
nor flimmering like the fell of beasts of prey

nor breaking out of all its contours
like a star: for there is no place
that does not see you. You must change your life.

translation by M.D. Herter Norton

Archaic Torso of Apollo

We cannot know his legendary head
with eyes like ripening fruit. And yet his torso
is still suffused with brilliance from inside,
like a lamp, in which his gaze, now turned to low,

gleams in all its power. Otherwise
the curved breast could not dazzle you so, nor could
a smile run through the placid hips and thighs
to that dark center where procreation flared.

Otherwise this stone would seem defaced
beneath the translucent cascade of the shoulders
and would not glisten like a wild beast's fur:

would not, from all the borders of itself,
burst like a star: for here there is no place
that does not see you. You must change your life.

translation by Stephen Mitchell

RAINER MARIA RILKE (1875–1926) was born in Prague and traveled extensively throughout Europe during turbulent times. In 1902 he moved to Paris and, for a time, worked as secretary to Auguste Rodin. As a young poet, Rilke's idea of inspiration involved finding a key visionary moment, but seeing Rodin's daily perseverance at work influenced Rilke and made him think about how to be more objective. This new approach is reflected in his two-volume work *Neue Gedichte* (*New Poems*) published in 1907 and 1908. "Archaic Torso of Apollo" is the opening poem to the second volume. Rilke's later masterwork, the *Duino Elegies,* was started in 1912, but he found himself stymied and unable to complete it; a decade later, Rilke brought this religious, mystical sequence infused with existential suffering into fruition. Shortly afterward, on hearing news of his daughter's friend's death, Rilke had another burst of creative energy and wrote all fifty-five *Sonnets to Orpheus* within a few weeks.

"Archaic Torso of Apollo" is a sonnet with a clear rhyme scheme. It's a poem powered by absence and presence, and it involves the transformation of inanimate object into animating subject and vital force. The M.D. Herter Norton and Stephen Mitchell translations are both marvelous; they both begin with *We,* and, although they take different pathways, they unite again at the ending. Norton describes a "head, / in which the eyeballs ripened," whereas Mitchell describes a "head / with eyes like ripening fruit." The translations diverge significantly in the next two lines where Norton, translating "Kandelaber" as "candelabrum," writes "his torso still glows like a candelabrum / in which his gaze, only turned low . . ." Although Norton appears to follow the German closely, I have difficulty visualizing a candelabrum turned low. Is she describing a moment when the lit candles of a candelabrum are blown out but their tips are still glowing? If so, it will be hard to turn the light back on and up in intensity for the ending. Mitchell innovates and replaces the candelabrum with a lamp, and that is a wonderful stroke. A lamp turned low can be turned up bright near the end. I also find Mitchell's phrasing stronger with "that dark center where procreation flared," in contrast to Norton's "to that middle, which carried procreation." Also, although Mitchell doesn't follow the rhyme pattern in the German, he finds a way to use rhyme and internal rhyme to give a sense of the music with "torso," "low," and then "so."

In the second quatrain, the "smile" in the poem is intriguing and powerful. Normally, with the head of a statue in place, one can say that the figure smiles, but how is it that a smile, in the Mitchell translation, runs through the hips and thighs? I don't know German, but using an online dictionary, I translated "im leisen Drehen / der Lenden" into "in the quiet turning / of the loins." Many ancient Greek statues present the figure with a turn at the waist, which adds a little tension and life. In my reading of the poem, Apollo, the god of poetry, has turned toward the genital center of his body, and that quiet turning elicits a smile. This reading of the passage is seconded by Norton's translation: "in the slight turn / of the loins."

The statue is now sexually alive, and there's the simmering raw energy of a wild beast just below the surface of the stone. Norton's "under the shoulders' translucent plunge" is lovely and erotic; her next line features the imagistic and sonically rich "flimmering," but the simile that follows, "like the fell of beasts of prey," feels attenuated and dated in diction. Nevertheless, that energy cannot be contained; in the last stanza, the god Apollo has animated the statue into a living force, and, in both translations, it bursts "like a star." Now the light has been turned up! And the voice of the living statue says, "there is no place / that does not see you." The person or people who came into a museum room to look at the statue are now the object of the living statue's gaze. Subject and object have reversed, and the living force of Apollo inside the statue says to the viewer, the reader: *You must change your life.*

This ending is beautifully rendered in Stephen Mitchell's translation. Throughout the sonnet, Mitchell has carefully choreographed the sounds with "gaze," "gleams," and "glisten," though he may owe a debt to Norton's earlier translation where she employs "glows," "gaze," and "gleams." Mitchell may not have fully conveyed "the slight turn / of the loins"; but he finds a way with "glisten like a wild beast's fur" to stay close to the unfolding progression of the poem. In the last line, Rilke has a period before the living statue speaks. Norton and Mitchell both follow that in English. The silence of a full pause on the last line gives even more power and authority to Apollo/Rilke's shocking ethical command.

Appendix

I want to offer, for classroom or other use, additional translation and poetry-composing prompts that will make this book a writing resource.

I believe each zone in this book can lead to a prompt for making a translation and/or writing a poem, though some possibilities are more obvious than others. Using Zone 15, a teacher can invite students to follow the example of Rilke's "Archaic Torso of Apollo," choosing a work of art as inspiration for an ekphrastic poem. Using Zone 4, students can follow Apollinaire and compose a visual poem in the shape of an object.

In Zone 1, I begin by presenting Tao Qian's "Drinking Wine (V)" with words in English under each Chinese character, the phonetics in Pinyin spelling, and three translations, and invite readers to make their own. It's good to have options, and I include here a poem by Li Bai (701–762):

Question and Answer in the Green Mountains

You ask me why I live in the green mountains;
I laugh and don't answer—I'm at peace.
Peach blossoms on flowing water go into the distance.
There is another sky and earth not among men.

translation by Arthur Sze

問	余	何	意	棲	碧	山
wèn	yú	hé	yì	qī	bì	shān
ask (you)	*me*	*what, how, why*	*wish, idea, meaning*	*dwell, live*	*green jade, blue*	*mountain/s*

笑	而	不	答	心	自	閒
xiào	ér	bù	dá	xīn	zì	xián
laugh (I)	*and, yet*	*no, not*	*reply, answer*	*heart, mind*	*self, naturally*	*leisure, tranquil*

桃	花	流	水	杳	然	去
táo	huā	liú	shuǐ	yǎo	rán	qù
peach	*blossom/s*	*flow/ing*	*water/s*	*far, deep, disappear*	*thus, so*	*go*

別	有	天	地	非	人	間
bié	yǒu	tiān	dì	fēi	rén	jiān
leave, other	*there is*	*sky, heaven*	*earth*	*no, not*	*person, people*	*in between*

Under each Chinese character are the Pinyin spellings and a word or words in English.

The situation in this poem involves two people: One person has left a city and moved to a remote, mountainous area, while the second person visits and asks why he has done this; the poem is the first person's response. Note that in a seven-character line of Chinese poetry, the caesuras are predetermined. One reads the poem 1-2 / 3-4 / 5-6-7, where the slant lines mark the pauses. I mention this because a student might want to use those pauses in their translation. What happens if the translator chooses to translate the poem in four lines, as I did? What happens if the translator chooses to translate the poem in eight lines, using one of the caesuras in the Chinese line to determine the location of a line break in English? What happens if a translation in English uses the entire space of the page to show where the silences are in Chinese? There are many possibilities; once students have translated the poem, invite each to write an original poem *that could only have been written* after making their translation. I envision this poem as a "writing through" of a translation.

For a final writing prompt, one can follow up on the discussion of Kobayashi Issa's haikus in Zone 6. Invite students to try writing a haiku in three lines, then in one line, and then writing many of them, with or without following the syllable count. Invite students to write with immediacy, in present tense, and with deep attention. Ask them to write fifteen to twenty-five haikus, and then, looking at the haikus written, see if there is one that stands out; look to see if several haikus are in conversation with one another. Print out the haikus and cut them out into small pieces of paper; move them physically around on a tabletop. What happens if they construct a poem with several haikus: which comes first? which comes second? which one is the ending? Maybe a larger poem is emerging? As Rilke says, live the questions now.

Glossary

assonance: the repetition of a vowel sound in nonrhyming stressed syllables close enough to be heard

caesura: a pause inside a line of poetry that marks a rhythmic point of division

couplet: two consecutive lines of poetry that function as a unit

crib: a word-for-word translation prepared for a writer translating a work written in a language they do not know

dactylic hexameter: in ancient Greek poetry, it consists of six metrical units per line, where the first four units are either dactyls (each dactyl is one long syllable followed by two short syllables) or spondees (each spondee is two long syllables) and where the fifth and sixth units, in consecutive order, are either dactyl and spondee or spondee and spondee

ekphrastic: adjective derived from *ekphrasis,* referring to a poem that draws inspiration from any work of art, including architecture, painting, sculpture, film, music, weaving, and dance

end-stopped: referring to a line of poetry where the syntax and meaning come to a conclusion at the end of a line enjambed: (the opposite of end-stopped) referring to a line of poetry where the syntactic unit continues to the next line without a grammatical break

Pinyin: since 1949, the standard system of romanized spelling for transliterating Chinese

quatrain: a group of four lines of poetry that form a stanza

radical: one of 214 visually prominent components of a Chinese character under which the character is listed in a Chinese dictionary

stanza: a basic unit of poetic lines organized by a specific principle, with blank space between each unit

tercet: a group of three lines of poetry that form a stanza

Poem Credits

"Library of Congress" by Arthur Sze first appeared in *The New Yorker,* October 20, 2025. Reprinted with the permission of Arthur Sze.

"Drinking Wine (V)" by Tao Qian, translated by Stephen Owen, appeared in *An Anthology of Chinese Literature: Beginnings to 1911,* edited by Stephen Owen. Copyright 1996 by Stephen Owen and The Council for Cultural Planning and Development of the Executive Yuan of the Republic of China. Reprinted with the permission of W.W. Norton & Company Inc.

"Drinking Wine (V)" by Tao Qian, translated by David Hinton, appeared in *Classical Chinese Poetry: An Anthology,* edited by David Hinton. Copyright 2008 by David Hinton. Reprinted by permission of Farrar, Straus and Giroux. All rights reserved.

"Drinking Wine (V)" by Tao Qian, translated by Arthur Sze, appeared in *The Silk Dragon II* (Copper Canyon Press, 2024).

"Duality" by Orlando White appeared in *Saad Na'ach'aah* (*The Art of Words*) (Sputnik & Fizzle, 2024). Reprinted with the permission of the author.

Excerpt from *Tao Te Ching* by Lao Tzu, translated by D.C. Lau (Penguin Classics, 1964). Copyright 1963 by D.C. Lau. Reprinted by permission of Penguin Books Limited.

Excerpt from *Dancing with the Dead: The Essential Red Pine Translations,* translated by Bill Porter/Red Pine (Copper Canyon Press, 2023).

Excerpt from *Tao Teh Ching,* translated by John C.H. Wu. Copyright 1961 by St. John's University Press. Reprinted with the permission of

The Permissions Company LLC on behalf of Shambhala Publications Inc., shambhala.com.

Excerpt from *Tao Te Ching,* translated by David Hinton. Copyright 2015 by David Hinton. Reprinted with the permission of The Permissions Company LLC on behalf of Counterpoint Press, counterpointpress.com.

"The Carnation" and "L'Oeillet" by Guillaume Apollinaire, translated by Roger Shattuck, appeared in *Selected Writings of Guillaume Apollinaire* (1971). Reprinted with the permission of The Permissions Company LLC on behalf of New Directions Publishing Corp, ndbooks.com.

Excerpt from *Homeri Opera,* vol. 1, edited by David B. Munro and Thomas W. Allen (Oxford University Press, 1920). Text courtesy of Perseus Digital Library Project (CC BY-SA 3.0).

Excerpt from the *Iliad* by Homer, translated by Robert Fagles. Copyright 1990 by Robert Fagles. Reprinted with the permission of Viking Books, an imprint of Penguin Publishing Group, a division of Penguin Random House LLC. All rights reserved.

Excerpt from *Memorial: A Version of Homer's "Iliad"* by Alice Oswald. Copyright 2011 by Alice Oswald. Reprinted with the permission of W.W. Norton & Company Inc.

"Three haikus" appeared in *Inch by Inch,* translated by Nanao Sakaki (La Alameda Press, 1999). Text courtesy of La Alameda Press and the publication *Inch by Inch.*

"31 [He seems to be a god]" by Sappho, translated by Guy Davenport, appeared in *7 Greeks.* Copyright 1995 by Guy Davenport. Reprinted with the permission of The Permissions Company LLC on behalf of New Directions Publishing Corp., ndbooks.com.

"31 [He seems to me equal to gods that man]" by Sappho, translated by Anne Carson, appeared in *If Not, Winter: Fragments of Sappho.* Translation copyright 2002 by Anne Carson. Reprinted with the permission of Alfred A. Knopf, an imprint of the Knopf Doubleday Publishing Group, a division of Penguin Random House LLC. All rights reserved.

"31 [He is more than a hero]" by Sappho, translated by Mary Barnard, appeared in *Sappho: A New Translation* (University of California Press, 1958). Copyright 1958 & 2019 by the Regents of the University of California. Copyright 1986 by Mary Barnard.

"31 [In my eyes he matches the gods]" by Sappho, translated by Jim Powell, appeared in *The Poetry of Sappho: An Expanded Edition, Featuring Newly Discovered Poems* (Oxford University Press, 2019). Copyright by Jim Powell 1993 & 2019.

"Sólo la muerte" by Pablo Neruda appeared in *Residencia en la tierra.* Copyright by Pablo Neruda 1935 & 1993 and Fundación Pablo Neruda.

"Nothing but Death" by Pablo Neruda, translated by Robert Bly, appeared in *Neruda and Vallejo: Selected Poems.* Copyright 1993. Reprinted with the permission of Beacon Press.

"Only Death" by Pablo Neruda, translated by Donald D. Walsh, appeared in *Residence on Earth* (New Directions, 1973). Copyright 1973 by Pablo Neruda and Donald D. Walsh. Reprinted with the permission of The Permissions Company LLC on behalf of New Directions Publishing Corp., ndbooks.com.

"Chapter 2, verses 8–13," translated by Marcia Falk, appeared in *Song of Songs: Love Lyrics from the Bible* (Brandeis University Press, 2004). Copyright by Marcia Lee Falk 1973, 1977, 1990, 1993. Used by permission of the translator.

Excerpts by Búffalo Conde, translated by Michael Wiegers, appeared in *Reversible Monuments: Contemporary Mexican Poetry,* edited by Mónica de la Torre and Michael Wiegers (Copper Canyon Press, 2002).

"I'm glad your sickness" by Marina Tsvetaeva, translated by Elaine Feinstein, appeared in *Marina Tsvetaeva: Selected Poems* (Penguin Classics, 1994). Reprinted by permission of Carcanet Press.

"I like that it's not me" by Marina Tsvetaeva, translated by Carol Moldaw, first appeared in *Narrative.* Reprinted with the permission of the translator.

"mot-macumba" by Aimé Césaire appeared in *Moi, Laminaire.* Copyright 1961, 1982 by Éditions du Seuil. Reprinted with the permission of the publisher.

"Macumba Word" by Aimé Césaire, translated by Clayton Eshleman and Annette Smith, appeared in *Lyric and Dramatic Poetry, 1946–82.* Copyright 1990 by University of Virginia Press. Reprinted by permission of the Rector and Visitors of the University of Virginia on behalf of University of Virginia Press. "Mot-macumba" by Aimé Césaire originally appeared in *Moi, Laminaire.* Copyright 1961, 1982 by Éditions du Seuil.

"We Never Stop" by Najwan Darwish, translated by Kareem James Abu-Zeid, appeared in *No One Will Know You Tomorrow: Selected Poems, 2014–2024* (Yale University Press, 2024). First published by *Cordite Poetry Review,* Australia (May 2016).

Excerpts by Inger Christensen appeared in *alfabet* (Gyldendal, 1981). Reprinted with the permission of Gyldendal Forlag.

Excerpts by Inger Christensen, translated from the Danish by Susanna Nied, appeared in *alphabet.* Copyright 1981, 2000 by Inger

Christensen. Translation copyright 2000 by Susanna Nied. Reprinted with the permission of The Permissions Company LLC on behalf of New Directions Publishing Corp., ndbooks.com.

"Mira Wears God's Clothes" by Mirabai, translated by Chloe Martinez, appeared in *Blue like My Beloved: Poems of Mirabai.* Copyright 2026 by Chloe Martinez. Reprinted with the permission of New Directions Publishing Corp.

"Mira Tells a Story" by Mirabai, translated by Chloe Martinez, appeared in *Blue like My Beloved: Poems of Mirabai.* Copyright 2026 by Chloe Martinez. Reprinted with the permission of New Directions Publishing Corp.

"Archaic Torso of Apollo" by Rainer Maria Rilke, translated by M.D. Herter Norton, appeared in *Translations from the Poetry of Rainer Maria Rilke.* Copyright 1938 by W.W. Norton & Company Inc., renewed copyright 1966 by M.D. Herter Norton. Reprinted with the permission of W.W. Norton & Company Inc.

"Archaic Torso of Apollo" by Rainer Maria Rilke, translated by Stephen Mitchell, appeared in *The Selected Poetry of Rainer Maria Rilke,* edited by Stephen Mitchell. Translation copyright 1982 by Stephen Mitchell. Reprinted with the permission of Random House, an imprint and division of Penguin Random House LLC. All rights reserved.

"Question and Answer in the Green Mountains" by Li Bai, translated by Arthur Sze, appeared in *The Silk Dragon II* (Copper Canyon Press, 2024).

Acknowledgments

I thank my editor Michael Wiegers for his visionary support. Michael brainstormed with me about possible texts and translations, and, as I developed a list, he also advocated for the humanizing power of translation. Thanks to Claretta Holsey for revising the introduction and for overseeing all aspects of production with such care and insight; thanks to Rowan Sharp and David Caligiuri for their remarkable copyediting; and thanks to Ryo Yamaguchi and to Elizabeth Brueggemann for ongoing, steadfast support.

Thanks to Carol Moldaw, Chloe Martinez, Orlando White, and Kareem James Abu-Zeid for help in shaping the discussion to their respective zones; thanks to Jennifer Rose for tracking down M.D. Herter Norton's translation of Rilke's "Archaic Torso of Apollo"; thanks to Kiana Rezakhanlou for suggestions regarding the discussions of Greek poetry; thanks to Sheng Yu for providing Pinyin spellings for the Chinese poems in Zone 1 and in the appendix. And special thanks to Rob Casper and to Aimee Hess and Hannah Freece at the Library of Congress for their commitment and ongoing support.

Index of Poets and Translators

About the Editor

Arthur Sze is the twenty-fifth poet laureate of the United States and author of twelve books of poetry, including *Into the Hush* (2025); *The Glass Constellation: New and Collected Poems* (2021), selected for a 2024 National Book Foundation Science + Literature Prize; *Sight Lines* (2019), for which he received the National Book Award; *Compass Rose* (2014), a Pulitzer Prize finalist; *The Ginkgo Light* (2009), selected for the PEN Southwest Book Award and the Mountains & Plains Independent Booksellers Association Book Award; *Quipu* (2005); *The Redshifting Web: Poems 1970–1998* (1998), selected for the Balcones Poetry Prize and the Asian American Literary Award; and *Archipelago* (1995), selected for an American Book Award. He has also published *The Silk Dragon II: Translations of Chinese Poetry* (2024) and edited *Chinese Writers on Writing* (2010). Another collection, *The White Orchard: Selected Interviews, Essays, and Poems,* was published by the Museum of New Mexico Press in spring 2025.

Sze is recipient of the 2025 Bollingen Prize for American Poetry for lifetime achievement, the 2024 Rebekah Johnson Bobbitt National Prize for Poetry, the Ruth Lilly Poetry Prize, the Shelley Memorial Award, the Jackson Poetry Prize, a Lannan Literary Award, a Guggenheim Fellowship, a Lila Wallace–Reader's Digest Writers' Award, two National Endowment for the Arts Creative Writing Fellowships, and a Howard Foundation Fellowship, as well as five grants from the Witter Bynner Foundation for Poetry. He is the first poet laureate of Santa Fe, where he lives with his wife, the poet Carol Moldaw. A chancellor emeritus of the Academy of American Poets and a fellow of the American Academy of Arts and Sciences, Sze was the 2023–2024 Mohr Visiting Poet at Stanford University. His poetry has been translated into fifteen languages, including Chinese, Dutch, German, Portuguese, and Spanish. He is a professor emeritus at the Institute of American Indian Arts.

POETS FOR POETRY

Copper Canyon Press poets are at the center of all our efforts as a nonprofit publisher. Poets create the art of our books, and they read and teach the books we publish. Many are also generous donors who believe in financially supporting the vibrant poetry community of Copper Canyon Press. For decades, our poets have quietly donated their royalties, have contributed their time to our fundraising campaigns, and have made personal donations in support of emerging and established poets. Their generosity has encouraged the innovative risk-taking that sustains and furthers the art form.

The donor-poets who have contributed to the Press since 2023 include:

Jonathan Aaron
Kelli Russell Agodon
Pamela Alexander
Kazim Ali
Ellen Bass
Erin Belieu
Mark Bibbins
Linda Bierds
Sherwin Bitsui
Jaswinder Bolina
Marianne Boruch
Laure-Anne Bosselaar
Cyrus Cassells
Peter Cole and Adina Hoffman
Elizabeth J. Coleman
Shangyang Fang
John Freeman
Forrest Gander
Jenny George
Dan Gerber
Jorie Graham
Roger Greenwald
Robert and Carolyn Hedin
Bob Hicok
Ha Jin
The estate of Jaan Kaplinski
Laura Kasischke
Jennifer L. Knox
Ted Kooser
Stephen Kuusisto
Deborah Landau
Sung-Il Lee
Ben Lerner
Dana Levin
Maurice Manning
Heather McHugh
Jane Miller
Roger Mitchell
Lisa Olstein
Gregory Orr
Eric Pankey
Kevin Prufer
Alicia Rabins
Dean Rader
Paisley Rekdal
James Richardson
Alberto Ríos
David Romtvedt
Sarah Ruhl
Mark Schafer
Natalie Shapero
Brenda Shaughnessy
Primus St. John
Arthur Sze
Yuki Tanaka
Elaine Terranova
Chase Twichell
Ocean Vuong
Connie Wanek
Emily Warn

Poetry is vital to language and living. Since 1972, Copper Canyon Press has published extraordinary poetry from around the world to engage the imaginations and intellects of readers, writers, booksellers, librarians, teachers, students, and donors.

WE ARE GRATEFUL FOR THE MAJOR SUPPORT PROVIDED BY:

academy of american poets

OFFICE OF ARTS & CULTURE SEATTLE

ARTSFUND

THE PAUL G. ALLEN FAMILY FOUNDATION

Hawthornden Foundation

POETRY FOUNDATION

INGRAM CONTENT GROUP

the point envision · enact · evolve

McSWEENEY'S

WASHINGTON STATE ARTS COMMISSION

ART WORKS. National Endowment for the Arts arts.gov

The Witter Bynner Foundation for Poetry

TO LEARN MORE ABOUT UNDERWRITING
COPPER CANYON PRESS TITLES,
PLEASE CALL 360-385-4925 EXT. 105

WE ARE GRATEFUL FOR THE MAJOR SUPPORT PROVIDED BY:

Anonymous
Richard Andrews and Colleen Chartier
Jill Baker and Jeffrey Bishop
Anne and Geoffrey Barker
Mona Baroudi and Patrick Whitgrove
Rick Shinsui Bowles
John Branch
Diana Broze
John R. Cahill
Sarah J. Cavanaugh
Peter Currie
Geralyn White Dreyfous
Bruce Easter
Mimi Gates
Claire Gribbin
Gull Industries Inc. on behalf of William True
Linda Healy
Carolyn and Robert Hedin
David and Jane Hibbard
Bruce S. Kahn
Phil Kovacevich and Eric Wechsler
Eric La Brecque
Maureen Lee and Mark Busto
Jembaa and Jason Mai
Ellie Mathews and Carl Youngmann as The North Press
Kathryn O'Driscoll
Petunia Charitable Fund and advisor Elizabeth Hebert
Suzanne Rapp and Mark Hamilton
Adam and Lynn Rauch
Emily and Dan Raymond
Joseph C. Roberts
Cynthia Sears
Kim and Jeff Seely
Tree Swenson
Julia Sze
Donna Wolf
Jamie Wolf
Barbara and Charles Wright
In honor of C.D. Wright from Forrest Gander
Caleb Young as C. Young Creative
The dedicated interns and faithful volunteers of Copper Canyon Press

The pressmark for Copper Canyon Press
suggests entrance, connection, and interaction
while holding at its center
an attentive, dynamic space for poetry.

English text is set in Archer and in Garamond Premier Pro.
Book design by Phil Kovacevich.
Printed on archival-quality paper.